Lovers Anonymous

By
Xavier Pierre Jr.

PriorityBooks
PUBLICATIONS

PO Box 2535
Florissant, Mo 63033
www.prioritybooks.com

Edited by: John L. Woodson
Cover Designed by Sheldon Mitchell of Majaluk
Photographer: Xavier Pierre Jr.

Manufactured in the United States of America

10987654321

Library of Congress Control Number: 2007932011

ISBN 13: 978-09792823-5-5
ISBN 10: 0-9792823-5-7

For information regarding discounts for bulk purchases, please contact Prioritybooks Publications at 1-314-741-6789 or rosbeav03@yahoo.com.

You can contact the author, Xavier Pierre at xavierpjr@gmail.com.

Lovers Anonymous

Published by Prioritybooks Publications
Missouri

Table of Contents

Preface

It's a strange thing to know that you are going mad. You can come to that logical conclusion by reviewing your own behavior after the fact, and sometimes even as you act, but a part of you is always utterly convinced that the things you do are what any normal person would do if placed in the same situation. My therapist told me to do the same thing over and over while expecting different results is the definition of insanity. That may be the definition, but to know that you are mad, and yet not know, all at the same time: that, to me, is the essence of madness.

In reviewing this book a reader might incorrectly conclude that the main character hates women. The truth is far more complex. I can't fully explain why I treated women the way I did during that period of my life, but at all times, even in my cruelest moments, I wanted to love women and I wanted them to love me. I was as addicted to women and sex as to alcohol and drugs and that was the problem. I don't pretend to be an expert and I speak only for myself but as an addict, the object of my addiction became exactly that: an object. Once this was the case, notions like respect, love or fair treatment became irrelevant. But if an object was found to be defective, it was simply discarded and replaced. I had no conscious reason to hate women. Up to that point in my life, no woman had ever really hurt me, at least not so deeply that I could justify the type behavior described in this book. No woman had ever humiliated me or betrayed my love. On the other hand, living in my own reality, I had every reason to be selfish. Everything I did was done to feed my ego, and everyone around me existed to satisfy my desires. It's clear to me now that I was trapped in an insane cycle of looking for love in a world of my own making where love itself couldn't possibly exist.

The pain, humiliation and rejection I had inflicted on my lovers is something I myself would experience many years into recovery, at a point in life where I could be philosophical about it, work out my resentment and move on without holding a grudge. In part, the writing of this book is a result of that process. Rather than blame, I chose to examine myself. I've been given the tools to recognize the pattern of insanity and I am empowered to choose. Every day I'm faced with choices. I'm still a work in progress but by the grace of God I choose sobriety and in most other matters, more often than not, I choose the way of reason.

The first step in writing this book was to actually live it. The events I write about were taken from the book of my life. There are many parts of the story that I sincerely wish had never happened but the simple truth is that no amount of wishing can make my past go away. I know, because I tried. The life I've lived is the history I'm stuck with. Having failed to make my past go away, I realized that I had no other choice but to make a "searching and fearless moral inventory" of myself and move forward from there. Fortunately, the story isn't over. I'm adding to it every day and I'm working hard to make it to a happy ending.

Since the last thing I want to do is cause more hurt to the many people who appear in this book, I've changed most of the names not only of people, but also of key places. Those who know me today, and even some who have known me for many years have asked, after reading initial drafts, "Xavier, did you really do those things?" Sadly, the answer is yes. Please note however that this isn't a documentary of my life, nor is it written like one. I've endeavored not only to tell my story of redemption, but to tell that story in a compelling way. From the beginning, I felt it was important to write a good book. To that end, I've taken certain liberties as an author. In almost every case this was done to make the book more readable or convey important insight. Also note that this book is written in the first person and from the decidedly warped perspective of the person I used to be.

I've also been asked about the graphic sexual content. All I can say is that I wrote this book the only way I knew how. The sex is included not to titillate, scandalize or shock, but in order to give the reader full access into the mind of a man obsessed with booze and sex. In fact, there are more references to and descriptions of drinking than sex. For those who read this book and remember only the sex, it's my humble opinion that you've missed the entire point in addition to some valuable life lessons.

In order to tell my story I had to reinvent myself as an author. This meant making certain decisions about what was most important and what was least important. Ultimately the truth is most important, while the myriad details surrounding the events I write about are clearly less important. In the beginning I struggled mightily with myself every time I had to move a line of dialog from the person who actually said it to another person, or when I moved an event from where it actually took place to a different location. But in the end, I had to accept that what is said is often more important than who said it and what happened is often more important than where it happened. As a consequence of this inner struggle I can say without hesitation that this work is an accurate recounting of my life story as seen through the eyes of a broken man in dire need of recovery. Having sought and found deliverance I attest that this book, though not perfect, is fundamentally a true story.

I want to recognize all the unsuspecting actors who contributed to this story, quite literally, with their blood, sweat and tears. Though unappreciated at the time, they played their parts as best they could on the stage of my insane reality and I owe each and every one of them an apology. But to some I owe a much greater debt which I can never fully repay. To all of you, wherever you are, I humbly ask forgiveness.

Finally I want to thank the numerous friends who gave valuable input during the writing of this book.

Peace and Love,
Xavier
May 29, 2007

Dedication

Because it never occurred to me that I could do it; because they believed I could do it; because I couldn't have done it without them and because I'm a better person for having done it. For these reasons and more I dedicate this book.

To Alicia:
for inspiring me to look at myself in the most profound way.

To Tammy:
for pushing me to tell the whole story.

Chapter 1
"Pain in the Neck"

I opened my eyes and saw nothing. It was pitch black. I was in extreme pain and I had no idea where I was. My heart started racing as panic set in. "Breathe, just breathe, nice and slow, deep breaths," I said to myself, measuring out the words as I fought against the terror. Okay, I had to start with the basics and work out a solution. "My name, what's my name?" I waited for an answer but none came. "What's my fucking name?" I screamed the words inside my skull and waited. A painfully long moment later the answer came: "Xavier! My name is Xavier." Damn! I'd been through this before but it never took me this long to remember my name.

I was lying on my back in a narrow space about two feet wide. Using my hands, I could feel broken glass on the bare wood surface I was lying on. Every movement caused extreme hurt everywhere, but the worst pain was in my neck and I had great difficulty moving my head. I had no idea where I was but whenever this happened, I usually woke up in someone else's bed. Several times, I had even woken up in my own room and not recognized where I was. It was always scary but this was infinitely more terrifying. For all I knew, I might be at the bottom of a mineshaft… or worse. Wherever I was, this was very bad. The panic started again as I considered the possibility that I had been buried alive. "Easy now, slow down, deep breaths." I had to remain calm. Half expecting to feel the inside of a casket lid I reached up into empty space. That simple movement hurt like hell, but I was relieved to find that I wasn't in a coffin.

"Okay, so where am I?" Nothing. I had to start with something simpler. "Where do I live?" I fought hard until slowly the pieces of my identity started to fall in place. "I live in New York." But as I thought about it I realized that was wrong. I hadn't lived in New York for years. "I live in Haïti." I fought the pain to gather more memories around myself like a naked refugee covering himself with whatever rags he can find. "I work for The Agency. I'm the M.I.S. Manager for the Haïti mission." As I lay there in the dark, trying to move my head as little as possible, I started to remember. "I must be in the Flamenco. That's it! I'm behind the bar." But that realization only led to more questions: How had I gotten there? And more importantly, where was Bryan?

To get myself up, I had to use my hands to keep my head in the least painful alignment. This meant I had to get up very slowly and without using my hands. Once I was standing I tried hard to see, but there was absolutely no light, just pure black. I was in pain, I had broken glass all over me, and I was exhausted from the effort it had taken just to get up. The only logical explanation was that this was a bad dream and I would just have to sleep it off.

After three years of being an almost nightly patron, I knew the layout of the Flamenco as well as anyone. I felt my way slowly from the bar to the restaurant. Following the wall I made my way to a table in the corner, very slowly pulled it away from the wall and lined up three of the chairs to make a bed for myself. Very gently, I sat in the middle chair and prepared myself to lie down. Again, I used my hands to hold my head in alignment to the rest of my body and I used my legs as a counter-weight. Several painful minutes later I was lying across the three chairs. Then I blacked out.

When I regained consciousness, it was morning and Bryan was standing over me. "Xavier, wake up, you have to go home."

"What happened?" I asked.

"I don't know," Bryan said. "I put you to sleep in the spare bedroom and went to bed. When I got up and looked around I found you here."

That just didn't make any sense. How had I gotten behind the bar? From the persistent pain I knew that was real, definitely not a dream.

Bryan had an unusual urgency about him. "Listen man, I don't mean to rush you but you have to get the hell out of here." He grabbed my arm to pull me up.

"Wait! I sprained my neck, go slow." Bryan, the best damn bartender I knew, had also been a medic so I figured I was in good hands as he helped me to my feet.

"Okay buddy," Bryan said, "all set; now you really have to go."

"Bryan," I said, "I hear what you're saying but I can't go anywhere. My neck is seriously hurt. There's no way I can drive. I have to call home and get picked up."

Bryan wasn't happy but he could tell I was serious. "Ok, let's go to the bar and I'll make some coffee."

I followed him in, walking very slowly. As I sat at the bar, Bryan placed the phone in front of me and went to make coffee. I picked up the receiver, dialed home and when I heard the maid's voice I said, "Mary, where's Nelson?"

"Mr. Pouchon! Where are you?" the maid asked.

"I'm at the Flamenco," I replied. "I can't drive. Tell Nelson to take a bus and come get me."

Mary had been our maid for so many years that we considered her family. She was about my age. Nelson, her husband, was our driver and handyman, but more than anything else, he was our bodyguard. Since my stepfather was the one who had introduced them, they had asked him to be the best man at their wedding and he had happily accepted. Now the whole 'Mr. Pouchon' thing, that was my mother's idea. She was always big on protocol so from the day we moved from the Long Island suburbs to Haïti, all staff were to refer to me as Mr. Pouchon and my little sister was Miss Poupette. It was all very surreal when I was initially subjected to this at age fifteen, but I eventually got used to it.

Nelson was on his way but it would be a while so I decided to try and figure out what had happened the night before. Bryan came back with coffee and I explained the situation. "My driver's on his way but I have no idea how long it'll take him to get here."

"Don't worry about it," Bryan said. The urgency was gone. "Anyway, I'm gonna start cleaning up."

"I'd help you," I said, "but I can't move my neck."

"It's okay," he replied, "besides, this is my mess." Bryan turned and went towards the kitchen.

I reached into my pocket and pulled out a pack of cigarettes and a gold lighter. I put the lighter on the bar, pulled out the last Marlboro and crushed the empty box. Needing a large dose of nicotine, I broke off the filter, dabbed the cut end on the tip of my tongue, and lit up. I inhaled deeply and took a sip of unsweetened black coffee before letting out a cloud of deep blue smoke. The instant buzz was welcome relief to my many aches and pains as I tried to survey the damage. Yes, it certainly was Bryan's mess, and what a mess it was. By the light of day it looked even worse than it had the night before.

The Flamenco was my spot. At least four nights a week I could be found sitting at the bar, playing dominos or dice. I started going there three years earlier when Bryan and Roland, along with their respective mates, Anne-Marie and Sophie, had bought the place. Bryan was a former Navy SEAL from California and his girlfriend Anne-Marie was from France. Roland, also from France, was a retired mercenary and Anne-Marie's older brother. He had spent many years fighting all over Africa, wherever the money was good. Roland's wife, Sophie, was from South Africa. I liked them all from the start and soon, Bryan and Roland were my best friends. I'd been there for a lot of stuff. I was there when Sophie left Roland, and I was there for the procession of Dominican girls that Roland claimed were each the love of his life.

More recently, I was living through the unlikely breakup of Bryan and Anne-Marie. I say unlikely because I couldn't believe that Bryan was serious about kicking Anne-Marie out, even though it had been a month already. Wondering if that was where I had gone wrong, I started to review the events of the previous night.

∽:∾

"Run for your lives! He's gone crazy!" Roland was yelling at the top of his lungs, but the patrons and staff needed no urging as they stampeded up the stairs and out into the streets. Roland rushed right past me as I sat calmly at the bar on the stool closest to the stairs. Bryan was still at it, breaking glasses and throwing the Flamenco's extensive CD collection around like so many Frisbees. Then he looked around and realized that he was alone. All alone, except for the fool sitting calmly at the end of the bar. Bryan came around, walked deliberately up to where I was sitting and sat on the stool next to me. Without turning to look at me he said, "What are you still doing here?"

"Well," I answered slowly, "I haven't finished my drink yet." After pausing to light a cigarette I added, "And I'll want another one after this, and you know you make the best zombies."

Bryan let out a heavy sigh of resignation, got up from the stool and went back behind the bar to fix a couple of drinks. Normally there would be music playing, but Bryan had trashed the stereo so the only sounds were the clinks of bottles as he expertly mixed up the drinks and the occasional crunch of glass under his feet. As he came back around I swallowed what was left of the drink in front of me in anticipation of a fresh one. Bryan's zombies were special; nothing at all like the drink of the same name in the official bartender's guide. The legend was that Bryan's secret ingredient was a voodoo spell given to him by a local witch doctor. That bit of lore was, of course, for the tourists, but one thing was certain: despite the drink's high alcohol content, all you tasted was a rich sweetness. It was like liquid caramel, but it packed a mean punch. When he was done, Bryan took his seat on the neighboring stool, slid the fresh drink in front of me, lit a cigarette and started sipping his own drink.

After a few sips I asked, "So Bryan, wanna talk?" It was obvious that my friend was having a bad night and I wanted him to know that even if everyone else was gone, I was there for him.

Bryan turned to me and I could see the seriousness in his face. "Xavier, I'm angry, very angry. In fact, I haven't been this angry in a very long time."

I looked around at all the broken glass then turned back to Bryan. "Well, I definitely see that. What got you so upset?"

Bryan's eyes were cold as steel as he made direct eye contact with me. His nostrils flared slightly, and his face was reddening. To prepare myself to be as supportive as possible, I broke eye contact momentarily to take another sip of my drink. As I did Bryan spoke: "Xavier, you have no idea how much you upset me tonight, do you?"

I almost choked on my drink. In an instant I sobered up as my mind connected the dots. I'd known Bryan for years; he was one of my closest friends. I'd seen him angry many times, but NEVER like this. Apparently, Roland (a hardened killer, Bryan's brother-in-law and business partner) had never seen him this angry either. And there I was, the object of his rage, sitting no more than twelve inches from him. I had no idea what I had done, but I knew I was in big trouble. I swallowed hard then said, "Me!? What the hell are you mad at me for?" I tried to sound calm but it was futile.

Bryan glared at me. "Why did you bring that woman in here?"

❧:❧

Despite my best efforts I couldn't remember anything between Bryan telling me he was angry and me waking up behind the bar. Earlier that evening, I had run into Bryan's girlfriend, Anne-Marie, and asked her to join me at the Flamenco. She had declined. After all, Bryan had banned her from the restaurant. I insisted because I didn't think it was that big a deal. Besides, Bryan was now fucking my ex-wife, Alice, and I wasn't upset about that. Even when my ex moved in with him and started tending bar I didn't let it get to me, as long as she kept her distance and didn't serve me. So why Bryan should be upset if I walked in with his ex-girlfriend didn't quite make sense to me. I mean it's not like I was fucking her or anything. I just figured if he saw her, he would kick Alice out and patch things up with Anne-Marie. I guess at some point when we were alone Bryan helped me figure it out. So much for playing matchmaker.

I wanted to ask Bryan a few questions but I had a funny feeling about the way he had been trying to rush me out of the place, so I kept them to myself. I'd get his version of the story in a few days when all this blew over.

Eventually Max, the Flamenco's security guard, announced that someone was outside for me. I made my way, very slowly, up the stairs and out to the car. Nelson was inspecting the vehicle. He probably assumed that I'd been in an accident. When he saw me he hurried to my side with a worried look. "Mr. Pouchon! Are you Ok?"

"I'll be all right," I said, "It's just my neck. Help me into the car." I handed him the keys.

Driving home was torture. Nelson's natural impulse was to get me home as quickly as possible. Every bump in the road made me feel as though we had fallen into a ditch. The only thing worse was the curves. I had to order him to go no faster than fifteen miles per hour. When I got home, Mary fussed over me and even Pop, my stepfather, put in his two cents. I spent the rest of the weekend expecting my sprained neck to get better.

By the time Monday morning came around, the pain was simply too much to bear. I called in sick and Nelson took me to the doctor, who decided to take some x-rays of my neck. The x-rays revealed I had fractured two vertebrae in my neck. "When did this happen?" the doctor asked.

"Friday night," I answered.

"And you waited this long to come in? You're lucky to be alive."

The doctor had a sad and grave look on his face. He looked like he wanted to say something else, but he didn't. He put me in a neck brace and ordered me to three weeks of bed rest, flat on my back. I was to have absolutely no movement for three weeks and even after that I had to take it slow. I thanked the doctor and left, and on the way home, I had Nelson stop by the store to pick up a bottle of rum, a six-pack of Cokes and a pack of Marlboros. The doctor was crazy if he thought a broken neck would keep me in the house for three weeks, much less in bed.

I actually did what the doctor said for a few days, but by day four I was going nuts. I had to get out of the house. I called the Flamenco to find out what was going on, and to my surprise Anne-Marie answered the phone. Apparently, the net result of the Friday night incident was that Bryan ended up asking Alice to leave and taking Anne-Marie back. After telling her as much as I knew of what happened the night Bryan went crazy, and giving her an update on my medical condition, I changed the subject.

"So," I asked, "what else is going on?"

"Well, actually we have a live band playing tonight," she answered.

Damn, I didn't want to miss that. "Really? Who's playing?"

"Remember Freddy, my daughter's boyfriend?" she said, "He

worked out a deal with Bryan. He'll be playing every Thursday night."

"That's pretty cool," I said. "Okay, Anne-Marie, see you soon."

"No you will not!" she snapped. "I'm not seeing you for another three weeks. You are staying in bed."

"Hey! Ease off," I said.

"Xavier, I'm serious," she insisted. "I don't want to see you until your neck has healed. Do you hear me?"

"Okay Anne-Marie, good talking to you," I said as I hung up the phone.

Anne-Marie was a dear friend and I knew she meant well but the last thing I wanted to hear was nagging. I thought about what I should do: stay home, in bed, on my back, moving as little as possible. Then I thought about what I wanted to do: go to the Flamenco, get drunk, bring home a girl and fuck her brains out. Then I thought of a compromise: stay home, get drunk but put as little stress as possible on my neck. The problem with the compromise was that I'd been doing exactly that since leaving the doctor's office. Fuck it! Compromises were for pussies. Besides, what was the worst that could happen? I would go to the Flamenco, sit at the bar and not move my head. Well, now that the issue was settled I needed to see to my transportation. I called Nelson to my room.

"Nelson," I said, "we're going out tonight."

"What do you mean Mr. Pouchon?" was his startled reply.

"I mean that I'm sick and tired of staying in this house," I said, articulating every word to emphasize that my mind was made up.

"But Mr. Pouchon," Nelson pleaded, "the doctor said you have to stay in bed."

"Screw the fucking doctor!" I shouted. "Now you can drive me or I can take a taxi, but one way or another, I'm going out tonight."

Nelson sounded desperate. "You can't be serious, sir."

I was getting impatient. "How much you wanna bet? And I'll even let you decide. You gonna drive me or do I take a taxi?"

Nelson looked perplexed. He couldn't bring himself to take me out against the doctor's advice, but there was no way he could let me take a taxi either. Finally he chose the lesser of the two evils. "Okay sir, I'll take you."

I could see he was conflicted so I tried to make him feel better. "Relax man, it'll be fine. And you'll be sitting next to me the whole time. What can possibly go wrong? Besides, we'll only stay out for a couple of hours."

"Okay sir, if you say so," Nelson answered.

We left the house around 9:00 and when we got to the Flamenco, the street in front of the restaurant was packed. Nelson double parked at the entrance and let me out. Max, the security guard, was very surprised to see me but he rushed to open my door and helped me out. I'd never seen a crowd like this in front of the restaurant before. Nelson started freaking out and asked me to wait with Max until he could park the car and get back to me.

When Nelson came, Max cleared a path to the head of the line while Nelson covered my back. Half-way down the hallway leading to the stairs that led down to the bar, there was a podium. Anne-Marie's daughter, Martine, was sitting behind it collecting the cover charge for anyone wanting to go downstairs. Martine, a petite little fox with an angelic face and brownish-blond hair that hung all the way down to her ass, was born and raised in France. She'd only been in Haïti about six months. Freddy, a local artist, was her boyfriend, and his band was scheduled to play that night.

When Martine saw me she said, "Xavier! What the hell are you doing here?"

"Are you kidding?" I said, "You really think I would miss this? I had to come and show my support." And with that I leaned forward and gave her a kiss and hug. "How much to get in?"

"Go ahead," she said.

"Thanks sweetie." I pointed to Nelson. "He's with me. He's my driver."

"Okay," she said, and waved Nelson in.

The show hadn't started yet but the bar was packed. As I entered, I could see a lot of surprised faces looking my way. Bryan was nowhere to be seen, but behind the bar there were three bar maids and Anne-Marie. The girl closest to Anne-Marie tapped her on the shoulder and pointed in my direction. Anne-Marie turned towards me with a distressed look but when she saw the big grin on my face she couldn't help but smile. Rather than shout above the crowd, she made a sign for me to meet her at the end of the bar. When I got to her, she hugged me and said, "Xavier, you have to go home. You're gonna fuck up your neck."

"Listen," I said, "I'm tired of staying home. Just park me here, keep the beers coming and I'll stay out of everyone's way. You can kick me out if you want to but I'll just go drink somewhere else. I'm not going home."

She could see it was no use. "Okay, but please just sit here and don't do anything stupid." She called one of the girls and gave some instructions. "Jacky, make sure he's always got a drink in front of him and don't let him out of your sight."

"No problem," Jacky said as she smiled at me. She then put a clean ashtray and a Corona in front of me I smiled back at her. "Okay sweetie, get me a double-shot of Jack Daniels to go with the beer and a pack of Marlboros," I pointed to Nelson, "and get him whatever he wants." With the important stuff out of the way, I turned back to Anne-Marie, "Before I settle in can I at least go look inside the restaurant? I haven't even said hi to Freddy yet."

"No!" she said emphatically. "I'll tell Freddy you're here."

I really didn't give a rat's ass about Freddy. I just wanted to check out the action in the restaurant but it was early and I'd get my chance soon enough. In the meantime, a few drinks would get me in just the right frame of mind.

I'd been sitting there for twenty or thirty minutes when a young lady climbed up on the stool next to me. "Hi there," she said, "my name is Pattie."

I had to turn my entire body to face her. In one glimpse I took her in. She wore a sleeveless t-shirt, tight jeans, and tennis shoes. Underdressed for the occasion, but she was a cute girl with a well-developed chest, a pretty face, and braids down to her shoulders. At most, she was eighteen but probably younger. "My name is Xavier," I answered.

"I know," she said, "I know all about you."

Surprised, I said, "Really, and what do you know about me?"

"Well," she started, "I know that you're very nice and charming, that you have a lot of girls after you, and that you're not with your wife anymore."

"Ex-wife!" I corrected, "I'm divorced."

"Sorry," she said, "ex-wife. And I know that you work for The Agency."

"Well Pattie, you really do know all about me," I said sarcastically. "Mind telling me how old you are?"

"Old enough," she replied defiantly.

"Old enough for what?" I asked.

"Old enough to be your girlfriend, old enough to take care of you, and old enough to satisfy you."

I couldn't help laughing. "And who told you I was looking for a girlfriend?"

"Just try me," she persisted, "and you'll never want anybody else."

"Look," I said, "you seem like a really nice girl, but I'm not looking for a girlfriend."

"Take me home with you," she said, "you'll see."

I laughed again. "So you want to interview for the position of girlfriend? What kind of experience do you have?"

"Like I said," she leaned forward, put a hand on each of my knees, and looked up into my eyes with what she probably thought was a seductive look, "take me home and find out for yourself."

Right about then, Jacky put another beer in front of me and waited for my instructions.

"Get a beer for my new friend Pattie," I said.

As though she knew what I was going to say, Jacky instantly produced another beer and put it in front of Pattie.

"And make sure my old friend Nelson is in good shape back there," I added.

"I'm fine sir," Nelson said as Jacky walked away.

My back was to Nelson as I faced Pattie. "What do you think of this girl Nelson?"

"I don't know sir," he said, "she looks awful young."

"Don't listen to him," Pattie said. "I'm all the woman you'll ever need."

The words coming out of this little girl were so ridiculous I had to laugh, but her boldness had me fascinated. Against my better judgment I reached for my wallet, pulled out a business card and turned towards the bar to write. "I'll tell you what Pattie…" I drew a line through my work number and flipped the card over. "…I'll give you my home number. Call me, but don't call in the middle of the night and don't call twenty times a day."

Pattie had a huge grin on her face. "I won't, I promise."

After writing my number, I turned to her. "Don't call my job and don't come to my job, EVER. Do you understand?"

"Yes," she said quickly, "I understand."

"Now there's one rule you have to follow if you wanna be my girl," I said.

"What's that?" she asked.

"Under no circumstances are you ever to talk to my ex-wife." I stared into her eyes with a look of deadly seriousness. "Do you understand?"

"Yes, sure I do," she started, "but I don't know her, why would I want to talk to her? She's not my friend."

"She'll come to you," I explained, "and pump you for information about me. She's dangerous. Whatever you do, don't talk to her."

"I'm not scared of her," Pattie said. "I can take care of myself."

This poor little girl didn't have a clue. If provoked, Alice would just as quickly stab her and feel no remorse. But the real danger was that Alice was as charming as she was violent. She was a master at seduction and bragged no woman had ever been able to resist her. During our three years together, I had several opportunities to see her in action. The woman was ruthless and efficient. But it wasn't just women who succumbed to her charms. Despite her sixth-grade education, Alice was a social engineer of the highest order who could manipulate her way into just about any place short of a U.S. military base. I knew by the next day, Alice would know this girl had approached me and would start planning her attack. This was fine with me since it would give her something to do and keep her out of my hair.

As the night wore on they kept the drinks coming, but they couldn't keep me nailed down. I eventually made it into the restaurant. A portion of it had been cleared to make room for the band and make space for a dance floor. I danced a bit with Pattie and some of the other girls. Poor Nelson almost had a heart attack. We ended up staying until the place closed, that much I remember. The ride home, getting into the house, getting into bed, I don't remember any of that. One thing was for sure: going out had been a bad idea. My stepfather decided that I needed to be watched more closely, so he called his sister for help.

Chapter 2
"The Caregivers"

The shower curtain rod was an iron bar firmly cemented at both ends into the concrete and stone walls. It would easily support my weight and I held it with both hands to steady myself. When I felt the cool water being poured over me I flinched at the unexpected sensation. One pitcher, then another, and another. With each pitcher, my body became more attuned to the coolness, then I felt the warm hands delicately soaping my back. In one hand a bar of soap, the other empty; each hand alternately went over my neck, my arms, and my back; worked down to my butt and down my legs. Straining against the natural desire building inside me, I tried to calm myself by thinking of wind blowing across a field of wheat. It wasn't very effective so I went over my to-do list, but my list consisted of one item: three weeks flat on my back and no pressure on my neck. I had to come up with something better, and fast. My stepfather; I imagined him passed out drunk on his bed, which in fact was how he was at that very moment. That worked and I was in control of my body again.

Up to now, Mickey hadn't said a word. "Turn around so I can do the front," she said softly.

Slowly I turned and faced her but I didn't make eye contact. Countless women had seen me naked but this was different. After all, Mickey was my cousin by marriage; she was family. My dear cousin had agreed to come take care of me and nurse me back to health. My stepfather had made the request and her mother had agreed. For several days now she had been feeding me, helping me in and out of bed, and generally waiting on me. All of it was completely unnecessary since the maid was more than capable and my needs were actually quite minimal.

Her presence may have been unnecessary, but it was very welcome. From the first time we had met a few months before, the attraction had been immediate and mutual. Whenever she greeted me she always made sure our lips touched, and more than once the maid had caught us staring and smiling at each other from across the house. But she was my cousin so I contented myself with fantasizing about her. Besides, she was only sixteen and I had more appropriate women to satisfy my sexual appetite. But how could I have predicted any of this? Breaking my neck, Mickey moving in to care for me, or even her soft hands gliding across my chest; it was all so unexpected.

My cousin was a pretty girl. Like most young Haïtian women living on the edge of poverty, she was lean and strong. She was only an inch or so shorter than me with long muscular legs. Her physical beauty was all natural; her hair was natural and braided in a way that actually made her look even younger than she was. The ribbons certainly didn't help. She wore an old pair of terry cloth shorts and a tube top that showed off her small, firm breasts, more so now that she was wet from the water splashing off my body. Water and soap suds dripped from her elbows onto the floor and her bare feet.

She stood in front of me, working her soapy hands over my chest and down my belly, avoiding my eyes as much as I avoided hers. As she worked her way down, there was nothing I could do to stop my erection. I was a little embarrassed and I could see her trying to suppress a smile. She crouched down and avoided my loins while working on my legs, but the sight of my penis dancing above her head was too much. I gave up trying to be good and decided to see exactly how far this would go. She hurried to finish and stood back up to rinse me off. I looked into her eyes and said, "Not yet, you have to finish what you started."

She really had started this; she knew I was perfectly capable of taking a shower by myself but she had insisted on bathing me. Mickey hesitated but I held her gaze. She sighed softly, sensually, and then looked down at my erection. She took my shaft in one hand, my balls in the other and worked up a lather.

After a few short minutes I said to her rather firmly, "Okay, rinse me off and take me to bed!" The urgency in my voice was unmistakable. If she wanted to stop what was about to happen, she had better have done it before we entered my room. I used the tone of my voice to make that as clear as possible.

She hesitated a moment and then looked into my eyes. Not shyly but deliberately. She knew what I wanted and she wanted it too. Mickey rinsed me off quickly and handed me a towel and I wrapped it around my waist without even bothering to dry myself. Stepping out of the shower, I grabbed my cousin by the hand and walked hurriedly to my room.

As soon as we entered, I removed the towel. Before I could do anything, she took it from me and proceeded to dry me off. Slowly and carefully, she worked around my body, lifting each arm and making sure I was thoroughly dry, then she put on and adjusted my neck brace. In that moment, my urgency ebbed; I felt like a shogun being catered to by a delicate geisha. Her care and concern touched me. When she was done, I put my arms around her and held her close as my heart raced with excitement. I let her go, leaned forward and our lips met in a kiss. I thought about how long I had wanted to taste those lips as my hands explored the tight body that had inspired so many fantasies. I turned her around so I could get a better feel. My hands cupped her firm breasts and played with her nipples until she moaned softly. Wanting to see her naked, I pulled the tube top over her head and pushed her shorts down to her hips. She shook her hips and the shorts fell around her ankles revealing, not the sexy bikini panties I expected, but an old pair of briefs with little flowers faded gray from too many washings. I was struck with a pang of guilt. Did I really want to do this? She was just a child.

With her back to me she bent down, picked up the shorts, folded them neatly and put them along with her top at the foot of the bed.

From behind, I wrapped my arms around her and squeezed for a moment frozen in time. It took a twitch of my penis pressed up against her ass to bring me back to reality. I moved one hand to her breasts and slid the other slowly down her firm, flat tummy and under the waistband of her panties. I inched slowly down feeling for pubic hair but not finding any, another pang of guilt struck me and I stopped. She cocked her head back and with eyes closed she opened her lips ever so slightly and exposed the tip of her tongue. Instinctively, I accepted the invitation and tried to lean forward to kiss her but the neck brace made it difficult. As I did, my right hand slipped a bit further down and found a few curls crowning her clitoris. She let out another moan as she pushed her hips forward to find my fingers.

Okay, I was going to take her but I would make it as special for her as I could. I would make this an experience she would remember the rest of her life. I whispered in her ear to remove the panties and sit on the edge of the bed. She complied immediately and after kneeling between her legs, I put both hands under her ass and pulled her as close to me as I could. The strain on my neck caused significant pain but I didn't care, I had to taste her. I worked my tongue up and down her slit but couldn't quite reach her clit. Still, she responded with little guttural noises and a gentle, rotating motion of her hips. After a few minutes the pain was too much and I let out a groan. She knew instantly that I was hurting and pulled away from me. I saw the worried look on her face. She was supposed to be taking care of me not making my neck worse. She held me by my shoulders and slowly we rose to our feet.

Turning us around so that my back was to the bed she said softly, "Please lay down."

I sat on the bed and she eased me to a lying position then I motioned to the nightstand. "Get a condom from the top drawer."

She handed me the condom and within seconds, I was ready. Carefully, she climbed on top of me and tried to fit me in her small opening. Getting inside her was surprisingly difficult but after a bit of effort I felt something give and the head of my penis finally made it past her inner lips. Another pang of guilt. Though only average in size, inside her I felt huge. I could see it was hurting her but she was determined to please me. As much as she wiggled her hips, I wasn't going any deeper so I made her stop and told her to use her mouth instead. She looked at me hesitantly. She obviously had never done that before and I could tell she wasn't comfortable with the idea.

"Come on," I insisted, "it'll feel good and you'll see it's not so bad." After a short hesitation she was about to move between my legs but I stopped her. "No, turn around, I want to do you, while you do me." I coached her into position as I removed the condom. Once in place, she started licking my penis, then put the head in her mouth. Her crude technique was effective enough to get me wildly turned on, but I knew she wouldn't be able to make me come. Trying to find her clit with my tongue required too much effort and put too much strain on my neck. I needed relief and I needed it fast. "Okay baby that's enough, help me up."

She was confused. "Are you okay?"

"Yes," I answered, "I'm fine but I want to get on top of you."

"No," she said, "you can't, you'll hurt your neck."

"Don't worry, I'll show you." And with that I had her help me up. I made her lie flat on her back and after putting on a fresh condom, I climbed on top of her. To take the pressure off my neck, I rested my forehead on her shoulder and guided myself inside her. Damn she was tight! I could tell she was in pain, but inside me something snapped and I pushed forward as far as it would go. She let out a cry and the obscenity of it all pushed me over the edge as I started to pump hard and fast. Completely possessed with lust I used her body to satisfy the sadistic desire that had suddenly taken hold of me. It lasted less than a minute but when it was over she was whimpering.

"Oh baby, I'm sorry," I said and started placing soft kisses on her face, neck and shoulder. "I'm so sorry." I was overcome with guilt and I was desperate to make it better so I said the only thing I could think of: "I love you."

She gasped "Oh," and after a pause, "I love you too," and she wrapped her arms around me. I had made it better.

Later that night, I convinced Mickey to come back to my room. I was tender and patient and I took my time finding what made her feel good until she achieved orgasm. I wanted her to spend the night with me but she adamantly refused. After a few hours, she went out the back door and across the lower courtyard to the servant's quarters.

A few days later, I was lying in bed with Mickey's head on my chest. We had just made love and were enjoying the coolness of the sweat evaporating from our bodies when there came a soft knock at my bedroom door.

"What is it?" I asked.

Nelson answered, "Mr. Pouchon, you've got company," and he added softly, "it's Miss Yasmine."

Damn. What lousy timing. "Okay, pay the taxi but give me a few minutes before you let her in."

I slapped my cousin on the ass. "Come on, get up, you have to go." She got up and slipped into her clothes then turned to leave. "Hey," I said, "come here and give me a kiss."

She leaned over, kissed me, and smiled slightly.

"Much better," I smiled back, "now help me up so I can take a shower."

While in the shower I wondered how I would split my time between Yasmine and Mickey. Then I realized there would be no splitting. Yasmine would have me to herself all weekend. Yasmine's real name was Alice. She was in her late twenties and had a degree in Psychology, but couldn't find work in her field so she took a low-paying job at the Ministry of Justice. Alice took the more poetic name Yasmine to piss off her father, whom she hated. As far as I was concerned, any name was better than Alice, since that was also my ex-wife's name.

My mother had worked briefly at the Ministry, which is where she met Yasmine and the two of them became fast friends. Mom had introduced me to Yasmine more than a year earlier in the hopes I would leave my wife to be with her friend. I really resented her for that and I had very little respect for Yasmine before I ever even met her. We talked on the phone a few times and met for coffee once. When I made it clear I was trying to make my marriage work, she wished me luck and never called again.

I'm not sure why I kept her number but when I finally divorced Alice, I was pretty much open to anything and decided to ask Yasmine out.

One thing about her that really appealed to me was that she was very educated and intellectually stimulating. Of course it also helped that she had a killer body. My plan had been to sleep with her, dump her, then tell my mom what an easy lay her friend had been. I figured that would teach them both a lesson. I had started with an invitation to dinner which Yasmine eagerly accepted. When she had asked where I was taking her, I just said, "Upscale, wear something nice." As I stood under the cool spray of the shower, the scene played out in my mind like a movie.

◈:◈

The large, two-story, French colonial house was located in a nice part of town. Yasmine came out the front door as I was stepping onto the porch. When I saw her I was stunned. She was wearing a sexy black skirt and a sheer top that showed off her gorgeous legs and breasts. Her proportions were perfect. There was no doubt in my mind she put a lot of effort into sculpting and maintaining her figure. My eyes followed the sinuous line of her legs down to a pair of sexy sandals with four-inch stiletto heals. Her feet were perfectly shaped and pedicured. I stared at them. The bright red polish had me completely mesmerized until she said, "You like my sandals?"

"Oh yes," I stammered, "I mean you look great." I was finally looking at her face. Her hair was beautifully styled and flowed over her coffee-cream shoulders, her eyes were bright and seductive, and her complexion was perfect, but the crowning touch was her winning smile. Not only was this no ordinary girl, but she was a lot prettier than I remembered. She was sophisticated and obviously spent a lot of time and money on her appearance. This would be interesting.

Since I hadn't told her where I was taking her, I decided that an upgrade was in order. My original intention had been to take her to The Flamenco or one of the other nice restaurants in Pétion-Ville, but I decided to really impress this girl. I extended both hands to her palm up, and she put both her hands in mine. I looked at her hands; again, the only word was perfect. Perfect hands, perfect fingers, perfectly manicured with the same bright red polish as her toes and perfectly soft. I pulled her gently towards me and kissed her on each cheek, then stepped back, "I'm glad you're ready, let's go." Since she could tell I was impressed with her appearance, that put me at a disadvantage and I couldn't allow that.

In the car, I decided to skip the usual charming banter and start setting the tone for the rest of the night. "I hope you like seafood."

"Yes I do," she replied.

"Good, 'cause I'm taking you to one of my spots." That was a lie. I was actually taking her to the Pétion-Ville Club. The PV Club was an exclusive resort hotel and boasted the only golf course in the capital. It was also where most foreign dignitaries and journalists stayed, so the food had to be good and they had to have seafood. But the PV Club just wasn't my style, so it would be easy to act bored and aloof. I much preferred the quiet elegance of the Villa Creole, which, in my opinion, was the best run hotel in the country. But for tonight the flash of the PV Club was exactly what I wanted. When we turned onto the private road that led to the hotel, she didn't even try to hide her surprise. "You're taking me to the Pétion-Ville Club!?"

"Yeah," I replied, "I hope you don't mind."

"Mind!? Are you joking? I've never even been there!" she gushed.

"Are you serious?" I said. "Well, you haven't been missing much, but the food is okay."

She was quiet the remaining few minutes to the hotel, but from the corner of my eye I could see a huge grin on her face. This would be so much easier than I thought. We hadn't even gotten to dinner yet and I was already disappointed. Well no matter, those feelings would only help me put more distance between her and me. An attendant directed me to a parking space right next to the entrance and I walked around to get Yasmine's door. I gave her my arm and we walked into the lobby. She was beaming as she took it all in but I pretended not to notice as we walked to the restaurant. At the entrance, there was an aquarium with a very large lobster in it.

"Wow," she said, "I've never seen one that big."

"Table for two," I said to the maitre-d without acknowledging her comment.

We were seated and I ordered a bottle of white wine. Our waiter handed us menus and walked away.

After taking a quick glimpse at my menu and pushing it to the side I said, "I'm having the grilled salmon. What are you having?"

"My god!" she said. "What currency is this in? These prices are outrageous!"

"Darling, don't be silly," I replied. "Just order what you want."

"Well actually the lobster isn't that expensive," she responded, "I'll have that."

Now I was annoyed. "Yasmine, if I take you out to dinner it's to eat and enjoy your company, not discuss prices on menus. So stop looking at the prices and just order what you want."

"I'm sorry," she said. "I'll have the lobster." She was clearly embarrassed.

This might be fun after all. I stood my menu on the table and in a flash the waiter was at my side. "I'll have the grilled salmon and the lady will have lobster."

The waiter looked at Yasmine, hesitated, then looked at me, "Are you sure monsieur?"

"Of course I'm sure," I replied. "If the lady wants lobster, the lady gets lobster."

"Yes monsieur but unfortunately there is only one lobster left, the big one in the tank."

"Perfect," I said, showing my annoyance by putting on my fakest smile, "then the problem is solved, isn't it?"

"Yes monsieur," the waiter said nervously, "right away," and he hurried off.

I turned back to Yasmine, "What is everyone's problem tonight? Is it too much to ask that we all just have a nice entertaining evening?"

Right about then the sommelier presented me with a small glass, poured some wine into it and waited for my approval. I held the glass up to appreciate the color, I sniffed it to gauge the aroma, then I took a sip and swished it around my mouth to get the full taste. I held it a second or two, then swallowed and nodded. The sommelier poured two full glasses, put the bottle on the table, took two steps backwards and then turned and walked away. I'd like to think it was in that moment that Yasmine decided she had to be my woman.

When the meal was over, I had the waiter box the rest of Yasmine's lobster and dessert. "Check please," I said to him and he hurried off.

I lit two cigarettes and handed one to Yasmine. "So, how are you enjoying this?"

"Wonderful," she said, "I can get used to this." She leaned back and took a long drag of her cigarette. As she exhaled, she looked around and said, "I can definitely get used to this."

Just then, the waiter came back with a box for Yasmine and presented me with the check. I looked at it, put it face down on the table and without hesitation reached for my wallet, pulled out five new hundred-dollar bills and laid them on the table. Yasmine's eyes widened. The waiter was about to take the money but Yasmine shouted "Wait!" and looking at the waiter said, "Can you please give us a moment?"

"Of course madame," the waiter said and walked to a distance several tables away.

"What are you doing?" I said calmly but obviously irritated.

"I want to see the bill," she said and snatched it up from the table. "$428! That's impossible; the lobster was only $17."

"Darling, that's $17 a pound. Now let me pay the man so we can go."

She was still in a state of shock but wouldn't let it go. "This bill can't be right."

"You must be joking!" I said. "That's it, we're done. Waiter!"

He rushed over. "Yes monsieur."

"We're done thank you." And as I got up from the table I handed him another $20. "Here, take this and my compliments to the chef."

"Thank you monsieur, please come again," and he rushed to pull Yasmine's chair out.

As we walked out in silence, I was thinking to myself that for all her lack of class, Yasmine was one bold and headstrong chick and I would thoroughly enjoy bending her to my will. Once outside, I turned to her. "Don't you ever even think about pulling a stunt like that again."

"I'm sorry," she said quietly, "I really am, but you don't understand. You just spent almost half my monthly salary on a meal. And you did it like it was nothing. I've never seen a guy do anything like that before."

"Maybe you've been dating the wrong guys," I said.

"I guess you're right," she responded.

"Anyway, let's go have a few drinks," I said.

Yasmine got close and looked up into my eyes. "Or we can skip that and go to your house."

I held her face with both hands, leaned forward, gave her a passionate kiss then pushed her gently back a step. "Don't worry, I have every intention of keeping you for the night, but I want a few drinks first." Without waiting for a response, I led her to my car.

When we finally got to my house, I wasted no time. Yasmine surprised me by being both passionate and skillful as a lover; so much so that I kept her the entire weekend. Breaking her was going to be infinitely more fun than originally anticipated. In the months that followed, she spent many weekends with me, but we almost never went out. Even when we did, I spent as little money as possible. I also made sure she knew I was seeing many other women.

∾:∽

I suddenly realized I had been daydreaming in the shower and hurried to rinse myself off. When I got back to my room, Yasmine was laying on my bed, wearing my robe.

"Hi baby!" she jumped up to give me a kiss.

"Hey! Easy there, watch the neck!" I snapped.

"I know you're hurt baby, I'm not stupid, I'm just glad to see you," and with deflated enthusiasm, "aren't you glad to see me?"

I decided to lighten up. "Sure baby, how can you even ask that? Don't I always tell you you're the best?" I reached around her waist, grabbed her ass, and with a rough squeeze of both cheeks, I pulled her to me. "How can I not miss that fantastic ass of yours?"

She broke free, stepped back, held the robe open, smiled, and said, "Baby look!"

I glanced at her perfect size Cs and said, "Yes baby, you have very nice tits, I missed them too, now help me into bed."

"Baby no," she protested, "don't you notice anything different?"

"No, I don't," I snapped, "so can I get into bed now? My neck is killing me."

But she wouldn't give up. "Baby, don't you see? The hairs are gone."

As I said, Yasmine had as perfect a body as I've ever seen, but she had a few stray hairs around her nipples. The last time she was over, I had made an insensitive comment about them so she had decided to show me the offensive hairs were gone. "Oh baby that's great!" I said with mock excitement. I even bent at the waist to give each nipple a quick suck. "Can I please get to bed now?"

"Okay," she said looking a bit disappointed, "but you'll just have to get up again."

My annoyance was getting the best of me and she was really starting to piss me off. Anymore of this bullshit and I'd have to send her home. "And why on earth will I have to get up again?"

She smiled sheepishly, "Because I have a present for you."

That caught me off guard. She would often bring me a chocolate bar or other candy, but I treated it as of little consequence, never as a present. I looked into her eyes, making no attempt to hide my suspicion. "A present? Why the hell would you get me a present? What's the occasion?"

She looked away, "It's nothing, I just wanted to show..." Her voice was cracking.

I took her hand and pulled her towards me, "I'm sorry baby, it's this constant pain, it's making me cranky." I held her for a moment. Then I kissed her on the forehead. I thought she was going to cry but she didn't.

She recovered her composure and started smiling, "Okay baby, close your eyes."

Despite my best efforts I couldn't help smiling back at her as I closed my eyes. "Okay, this good enough?" I could hear shuffling noises.

"Yes baby," she replied, "just a few more seconds," and after a bit, "okay, open your eyes."

When I opened my eyes, there was a large gift-wrapped box on my bed with a large bow. For a moment, I didn't know what to say.

"Well, don't just look at it, open it," she said.

I approached the box and started carefully removing the tape from the ends.

"Come on, just rip the paper off!" she said. "I'm dying to see the look on your face when you see what I got you."

"This is my present," I countered, trying to buy time, "and I want to savor this moment." I winked at her.

She was glowing, "Ohhhhhh, that's so sweet."

Finally, I had the paper off and I opened the box. It was a new robe. All I could say was, "Wow!" and after a few seconds, "Baby you didn't have to…"

She silenced me with a finger to my lips. "Don't say anything. I just want to show you how much you mean to me. You're very special Xavier." And after a gentle kiss she said, "Well, put it on." She loosened the towel from around my waist and helped me with the robe. It was nice, really nice.

I turned to her, "Thank you baby, I really appreciate this… and I appreciate you."

She was beaming as she moved in close to give me a long, wet kiss. "Let me help you into bed."

She helped me get comfortable, then let my old robe slip off her shoulders and onto the carpet. Wearing a black thong and nothing else, she stepped back and slowly turned in place so I could admire her naked form. Next, she came to me and started kissing my face. She placed soft kisses every few inches, going down my body, all the way to my feet.

When she was satisfied that she had covered all of me and I was ready, she took a condom out of the nightstand and put it on me. After slipping out of the thong, she climbed on top of me. I slid inside her effortlessly and she started to grind. She kept up a nice slow tempo for a few minutes until her own desires urged her to go faster. She tried to control herself but that became more and more difficult, until it was altogether impossible. She had wanted to please me first, but what she would never know was that my desire had already been satisfied an hour earlier. Then Yasmine came with a force that shook the entire bed. She tried to keep quiet but her efforts were in vain. The entire house heard her cries of ecstasy.

She was about to collapse on top of me when I said, "Hold on, I have something for you too. Help me up." I had her lay on her back and I got on top of her with my head on her shoulder. As I entered her, I couldn't help thinking what a perfect fit she was. I started pumping at a slow, steady rhythm. At random, I would stop pumping and grind, but soon went back to pumping.

After a few minutes, she yelled "Oh my god! This is amazing!"

Steadily, I picked up speed until our combined cries were echoing through the large house and escaping from every open door and window as we collapsed in a sweaty heap. I was exhausted and my neck was really hurting now. Yasmine helped me get comfortable and after the obligatory cigarette, we dozed off.

I wasn't sure how long we had been sleeping when Nelson came knocking softly on my door. "Mr. Pouchon, you have another visitor. It's Miss Natasha. I tried to tell her you won't see her but she refuses to leave."

"Where is she?" I asked

"She's outside the gate sir," Nelson replied.

"Let her in," I said, "have her wait for me in the living room." I gave Yasmine a gentle shake. "Baby, help me up. I'll be right back."

Yasmine helped me to my feet, looked me in the eyes and said with a smile, "Tell your little friend that she can have you anytime from Monday to Thursday, but the weekends are mine, okay baby?" Without waiting for a reply, she kissed me and gave my balls a gentle squeeze before climbing back into bed.

I stopped in the bathroom to wash my face, and then I went upstairs. The living room was thirty feet long. I entered from the kitchen and Natasha sat on the large, red couch at the opposite end. She was wearing her school uniform and had her book bag next to her. When she saw me, she looked scared. I took two slow steps into the large room, then stopped and held my arms out to her. She sprang to her feet, nearly ran the distance, and helped me across the room to the couch.

"Are you okay?" she asked. "I missed you. Why didn't you tell me you had an accident?"

I ignored her questions but I noticed her brow was crowned with beads of sweat. I knew she had walked the three miles from the main road to my house. I yelled for the maid, "Mary!"

"Yes Mr. Pouchon," Mary yelled back from the lower courtyard.

"What kind of house is this? Get Miss Natasha some water." I ordered.

Mary yelled again, "I'm washing and my hands are full of soap. I'll send Miss Michele."

I turned to Natasha, "Would you prefer a beer?"

"No thanks," she replied, "water is fine."

A few minutes later, Mickey came with a glass and a pitcher of water on a tray. She presented the tray to Natasha, who held the glass as Mickey poured.

"Thank you," Natasha said, then began to gulp the water.

Mickey stood silently with the pitcher still in hand. I tried to make eye contact with her, but she just looked down at the floor in front of her.

"Natasha, Michele is my cousin," I said.

Natasha held out the glass for more water, "Really? Well, I'm pleased to meet you Michele."

Mickey didn't respond; she just poured more water and waited for Natasha to finish.

"Thank you," Natasha said, putting the empty glass on the tray.

Mickey turned and walked away. Her eyes had been lowered the entire time. I'll take care of her later, I thought to myself. Then I turned to Natasha. "How you been? How's school?"

"Fine, I graduate this year," she said. "How's Pop?"

"He's good," I said, "probably fast asleep."

When I met Natasha, she was working as a server in a club. At the grand opening I saw this hot chick behind the bar and made my move. Before the night was over I had her half-drunk and I had popped all but one button of her denim skirt. The owner wasn't amused but I came every night and spent more money than anyone else, so he put up with it. After a week, she was fired. When I asked her why, she told me the owner found out that she was only sixteen. Sixteen! What the hell was she thinking? Here we were, two years later, and Natasha was still hoping she could be my girl.

I shook my head to stop the flow of unwanted memories. "Listen sweetie, I know you came a long way but I really can't see you right now. Come back during the week, okay."

Right about then, Yasmine came and stood in the doorway, wearing just my old robe. She struck a pose, holding the doorframe above her head. "Hello!" she said with a smile.

"Hi," Natasha replied in a barely audible voice.

"Xavier honey," Yasmine was looking right at me, "don't forget what I told you, okay sweetheart?"

I couldn't help laughing, "I got it, I got it," then I added in a gruff voice, "Get your ass back downstairs."

Yasmine turned dramatically and left the door open so we could see her hips swaying as she walked away. The woman had balls; I had to give her that.

Natasha was clearly hurt. "Xavier…" She tried to speak but couldn't. I put my arm around her but she was still hot and sweaty from the long walk. I pulled my arm away and turned to face her. I reached out, took her chin and pulled her face to mine. I intended it to be a mercy kiss but Natasha saw it as her opportunity to show me what she had to offer and enthusiastically searched for my tongue with hers. My body kicked into auto-pilot. With no conscious thought on my part, my hands locked on her breasts then focused on the erect nipples poking through her uniform. When I heard her moan I reached up under her skirt and slid my hand under the waistband of her panties with one fluid motion. Natasha leaned back and spread her legs. I found her clit and wasted no time. I shoved two fingers into her opening and rubbed her clit with my thumb. The door was still open but I didn't care.

"Aaaaah!" Natasha moaned loudly with her eyes closed. She felt her way to my crotch, and found my penis only half erect. Hoping to get a reaction, she squeezed gently.

She got a reaction, but not the one she expected. I pulled my hand out from between her legs and rose painfully to my feet. "You have to go. I'll get Nelson to drive you to the main road." And with that, I started to walk away from her.

She got up and moved to block my path, "Xavier what's wrong? Honey, please don't do this to me! Whatever it is I did, I'm sorry. Please, Xavier, I love you!" She was crying hysterically.

"Oh good grief girl, get a grip!" I shouted. "You didn't do anything. Just come back during the week."

I suddenly felt very sorry for her so I put my arms around her and she buried her face in my chest, still sobbing. I just held her until the crying stopped.

"I'm sorry," she said.

"It's okay," I said as I led her into the kitchen. "Hang on." I grabbed two beers from the fridge. "Okay, let's go."

She helped me down the stairs to the lower level. I led her into the bathroom, put the beers on the counter and closed the door behind us. After washing my hands I stepped back to give her access to the sink.

"Wash your face," I ordered. As she bent over the sink to wash her face, I stood behind her. Without thinking I grabbed her hips and began to grind on her ass.

She raised her head and pushed back from the sink. "Oh yes, give it to me. Xavier honey, I want you so bad!"

She started to hike up her skirt but I grabbed her wrists. "No! Come back during the week." I released her, opened the bathroom door, grabbed the beers and stepped out. "Nelson!" I yelled, "Drive Miss Natasha to the main road."

"Yes, Mr. Pouchon," he yelled back from the lower courtyard.

"And get me a pack of cigarettes and more beer on your way back," I added.

I turned back to Natasha, gave her a quick peck on her still wet cheek, and wiped my mouth with the back of my hand. "I'm going back to bed. Just grab a towel from the cabinet." I turned and started away with the two beers.

"Bye Xavier," she said. "Please tell Pop I said hello."

Without responding I opened the door to my room, walked in and closed it behind me. I could hear Nelson talking to Natasha.

Yasmine was sitting on the bed, smoking a cigarette. "Xavier I can't believe you."

I handed her a beer. "What?"

"She's just a school girl," she said.

"I know," I replied, "I keep telling her that, but she just won't listen. I've been trying to get her off my dick for over a year. Anyway, she's gone now, so you have me all to yourself. Light me a cigarette, and help me to bed, my neck is killing me."

Chapter 3
"The Trap"

Saturday was a quiet day and there were no surprise visitors. I was kept pretty well sedated with plenty of booze, and Yasmine entertained me between naps. Pattie called several times, but I told Mary to take a message. My new girlfriend would have to wait her turn.

Sunday afternoon, Yasmine left. She had to be at work the next morning so I had Nelson drive her to the main road. As soon as the car left the front gate, I went looking for Mickey. We hadn't talked much since Yasmine came over and I knew her feelings were hurt. I brought her back to my room and explained that I didn't care about Yasmine and I was only using her for sex.

I told Mickey I loved her, wanted to be with her and that I wanted her to move in permanently. Since she had taken a week off school to stay with me, I offered to pay for her to go to a school in my neighborhood. To her credit, Mickey didn't go for any of it. Realizing nothing I said would make her stay, I switched gears and talked her into having sex with me. When we were done, Mickey retired to the outside quarters to wash up and pack her bag. Nelson would be taking her home as soon as she was ready.

After Mickey left, I took a shower and tried to take a nap, but I was so restless I couldn't sleep. I went upstairs to the family room to see if I could find a movie to pass the time. I had watched every movie in our collection at least once, so I dropped that idea. Then I found some science-fiction novels on the bookshelf and picked the one that looked the most interesting.

The family room was the largest room in the house. At one end, there was a pair of large double doors. This was the main entrance. Our house was at the highest point on a hill overlooking a valley.

Our front yard consisted of four grassy terraces leading down to a large parking area. Beyond the parking area was more grass, an almond tree, and a path leading back around to the lower courtyard. At the other end of the family room was a door that opened onto the upper courtyard. Along the side wall of the family room were two arched openings, one leading to the living room and one leading to the formal dining room. The living and dining rooms shared one large space. An interesting design touch was that the wall of the family room was straight throughout the entire length of the living/dining room, but curved into the large eat-in kitchen. My mother designed this house specifically for entertaining large groups of people. This was, after all, her dream house.

I put the book on the round table that served as the centerpiece of this half of the family room and walked from one room to the other. I imagined the house full of guests drinking and participating in all sorts of conversations, from political intrigue and the latest gossip at the Presidential Palace to discussing the business dealings of the rich and powerful families that controlled the country. As I stood in one of the arches daydreaming, my stepfather's footsteps coming up the stairs brought me back to reality. My mother's dream house had become a den of drunken debauchery for two men trying to escape their respective realities.

I walked to meet my stepfather as he reached the top step and kissed him on the cheek. "What's up Pop? Did you sleep well?"

"Are you kidding?" He looked a bit upset. "Who could sleep with all that noise your girls were making?"

Pop's room was right next to mine, but I honestly thought he'd been too drunk to hear or care. "I'm sorry Pop." I was genuinely embarrassed.

My stepfather continued as we walked to the round table. "And for Pete's sake, stick a sock in Yasmine's mouth next time, the girl kept screaming the whole weekend. At least Mickey had the decency to keep it down."

At that, I stopped in my tracks and said, "You knew about Mickey?"

"Of course I knew," Pop replied. "Do you think I'm stupid?"

I fought to keep my composure as I tried to explain, "Pop, I am so sorry. I never meant to…"

Pop interrupted me. "Forget about it. But I have to say, you're one hell of a stud. How many girls did you have this weekend? Five? Six?"

Pop seemed to be taking pleasure in embarrassing me and I didn't like it one bit. "Pop, it wasn't anything like that."

"The hell it wasn't!" he interrupted again. "You had girls practically bumping into each other."

"Pop, can we talk about something else?" I asked.

We sat at the table and Pop's voice got sad. "Poor Natasha. She's a nice girl."

Pop liked Natasha from the first day he met her. She had come to visit me one day when I wasn't expecting her. Pop kept her company and they just talked and laughed until I came home a few hours later. From that day, she always made sure she spent a little time with him whenever she came over. Things like that meant a lot to Pop.

"Pop, let's be serious," I said, "she's still in school."

Pop was serious as he looked at me. "That hasn't stopped you from sleeping with her though, has it? Anyway, I still think she has more class than any other girl you've dragged into this house."

I couldn't believe we were having this conversation. "Okay Pop, I'm gonna go take a shower now."

Pop wasn't buying it. "You just took a shower."

I had to hand it to him, he didn't miss a thing when he was sober. But this was too much. I had to get the hell out of there. "Well, let me tell Mary you're up so she can fix you a plate." With that, I grabbed my book and went downstairs. On the way, I yelled for Mary to serve Pop dinner and bring me a rum and coke.

I retired to my room feeling somewhat foolish, but by my reckoning, the weekend had turned out pretty good. My only complaint, besides being left alone, was that my neck hurt like hell. I tried to read my book, but thanks to Pop I couldn't get Natasha out of my head. As I lay there, the flood of unwelcome memories intruded on what little peace my tortured mind could forge, so I gave up on reading and did what I did best. A few hours and many rum and cokes later, I fell from a mindless stupor into a semblance of sleep.

Monday morning started out with a breakfast of straight rum with a beer chaser; whatever it took to stay conscious as little as possible. Later in the afternoon Nelson announced that Natasha was there to see me. By then, I was pretty well lit. I told him to bring her to my room along with a couple beers.

"Hi," she said as she entered.

"Hey there," I answered.

After dropping her book bag by the door, Natasha put the beers on my desk, came to the edge of my bed, leaned over and kissed me gently on the lips. "How are you?" she asked.

"I'll live," I answered, "but I'll feel much better after you hand me that beer."

Natasha turned to the desk, grabbed one of the bottles and handed it to me. She was about to sit in the chair next to my desk.

"Sit here next to me," I said. "The other one is for you, aren't you thirsty?"

"I'll have it in a bit," she said as she positioned herself on the edge of the bed. "Pop isn't home from work yet?"

"No he isn't," I answered as I put my hand on her lap. "He'll be home in an hour or so." I slid my hand under her mini-skirt as I stared at her breasts bulging through her tight top. "Didn't you go to school today?"

"Yes," she answered, "my uniform is in my book bag. I wore this for you."

I looked in her eyes and saw the longing, that pathetic look of blind love. "Why don't you take off your clothes?" I said. "You can take a shower if you want." I figured she could probably use one after walking so far.

"No, that's okay," she said.

I closed my eyes and moved my hand further up her skirt. The soft skin of her thighs was moist with sweat. I moved up to her panties, brushed her outer lips through the material and predictably, her legs spread apart to allow me full and complete access.

It had been almost a year since we last had sex. I had decided that this girl was simply too much trouble and I had cut her off. Or at least I had tried to, but here she was, determined to have a relationship with me. Natasha was a beautiful, intelligent girl from a close-knit family with a very bright future ahead of her. If she used half the brain God had given her, she would have given up on us a long time ago, but she was desperately in love with me and that annoyed me beyond description.

I toyed with her but I didn't put my hand inside her panties because I knew that's what she wanted me to do. With my eyes still closed I stopped, took a sip of my beer, then traced a line down her thighs and caressed her knees. I was determined to stick to my decision not to have sex with her, but I was taking sadistic pleasure in teasing her like this. That would prove to be my undoing.

"Xavier," she said, "I really miss making love with you."

I took another sip of beer. "Really? And why is that?"

"No one has ever made love to me the way you do," she answered.

"I told you it was over between us ages ago." I reminded her.

"Why?" she asked, "that makes no sense. We were happy together. Why can't you remember that?"

I opened my eyes and glared up at her. "You know what? Go home. Get the hell out of here." I took my hand off her knee. "I don't need this shit!"

"Oh baby no!" she begged. "I'm sorry; I didn't mean to upset you. Please, Xavier, don't make me go. Do anything you want to me, but don't make me go. Please honey, I'm begging you. I'll do anything for you."

Hearing those words caused a reaction in me so spontaneous that it caught me completely by surprise. A wave of desire surged from deep inside my body and I felt the blood rush to my penis in an immediate erection. Natasha was moving to her knees even as she was speaking. Kneeling next to the bed, she looked into my eyes with the pleading look of a woman begging for her life. At first she was afraid to touch me for fear of my response, but the sudden bulge in the sheets caught her eye. She turned to see what it was and knew instantly I was hard. At that point, she knew she had nothing to lose, so she reached out and touched my erection through the sheets. The feeling was electric. I closed my eyes and she continued to massage. Seeing that I wasn't stopping her, she slowly pulled the sheet away and uncovered me. Now that she was free to better stimulate me, she went slowly at first, afraid to do something wrong. Then suddenly, I felt what could only be her mouth on the head of my penis.

She sucked for a few minutes before slowing down so she could speak. "Baby," she said. Gentle sucking. "I want to make you feel good." Gentle sucking. "I want you to feel yourself inside me." Gentle sucking. "You don't have to do anything." Gentle sucking. "I just want to take care of you." Gentle sucking. "Please baby, just let me do that for you. I won't ask for anything else." Gentle sucking.

I had to admit, she was pleading her case exceptionally well. "The nightstand, look in the drawer and get me a condom," I ordered.

That was all she needed to hear. While she rifled through the drawer, I finished my beer and dropped the empty bottle on the carpet. "Hurry up before I change my mind!" I said harshly.

She turned and looked at me with a sick, distressed look. "I can't find any. Is this the only place you keep them?"

I did some quick math and realized that what she said was entirely possible. Between a week of Mickey and a weekend of Yasmine, I had gone through a box of twenty-four condoms. "Sorry, I guess I'm out. But you can always make me come with your mouth. You were doing pretty good there."

She tried to hide her disappointment and immediately started sucking again. After a few minutes, she stopped and quickly stripped out of her clothes.

"What are you doing?" I asked.

"Nothing honey, just getting more comfortable. Here, I'll get another one later." She handed me the other beer, climbed onto the bed and took a position between my legs. Bracing herself with a hand on each of my hips, she teased the head of my penis with her tongue, then put her head between my legs and sucked on my balls.

"Damn!" I said, almost chocking on the beer. "That felt great, but warn me next time."

She ignored me and started to lick a path from the base of my penis, up the shaft and back down again. "Finish your beer baby," she urged.

She had a point; I had better things to do with my hand than simply hold a beer. I put the bottle to my mouth, she put my dick in hers and as I guzzled, she slurped. The feeling was delicious. When the bottle was empty, I let it drop to the carpet and heard it clink against the first bottle.

Realizing I was done, Natasha started kissing a path up my belly. As she did, she reached up, grabbed each of my nipples and gave then a pinch. Slowly she slid onto my body until she was lying on top of me. When her lips were close to mine, we found each other and our tongues explored one another's mouths. Even as I tasted myself, I wanted her so badly. I could feel my dick between her legs. It would be so easy, but I couldn't let that happen. I just didn't need that kind of guilt on top of all the other baggage I was carrying. In anguish, I bit her lower lip and held it between my teeth. This seemed to excite her even more and she reacted by grinding her clit on the head of my dick. When I released her lip a second or two later, she pushed herself up, straddled me, grabbed my shaft and pushed the head in her wet pussy.

"What the fuck are you doing? Stop!" I yelled. But I slipped easily inside her.

"Baby, please," she pleaded. "Just for a few minutes, then I'll get off."

"Get off now!" I yelled, but there was no stopping her. She started to rock her body back and forth in a slow rhythm.

"Get off now!" My words fell on deaf ears. Natasha was in a trance.

She closed her eyes and cocked her head back as she kept a perfect rhythm with her back and forth rocking. I had to admit, the feeling was pure delight. As I looked up at her, I allowed myself to admire her beauty. Natasha was only eighteen but she was all woman. Like Marilyn Monroe, she had meat on her bones. Her hips were wide, her butt was well-rounded, her thighs were generous, her breasts were full, but her body was tight.

Looking up at her, I admired her beauty. The features of her face were hypnotizing me. Her delicate nose, her soft cheeks, her pretty eyes closed to better release her other senses, her pouting lips, forming a silent "Oh."

All of it came together. I should have stopped her. If there was anything decent in me and for all that was human, I should have stopped her. But I was overcome by the sensual torrent and I admitted defeat. "Okay, but when I tell you that I'm about to come, you have to get off me, alright?"

She had ignored me up until then but without hesitation she said, "Yes baby, I'll get off."

Satisfied with her answer, I relaxed to enjoy the ride. Gently, she started picking up the tempo. I was hoping to make this last, but within minutes I was on the verge of climax. It wasn't sudden, but the way it was building up I could tell it was going to be huge.

"Okay, you'd better stop, I'm almost there." No response.

"Natasha, I'm close." No response. "I'm not kidding, get off!" Still no response. Holy shit, she wasn't gonna stop! I tried to push her off but when I did, she leaned forward, wrapped her arms and legs around me, and started bucking wildly with her hips.

I screamed, "No!" but the volcano that had been building pressure inside could no longer be contained. The eruption was massive. "Oh fuck! Fuck!" Even as I screamed, I could hear her screaming right along with me. She was having a massive orgasm of her own.

When it was over, we just lay there in a tired heap.

After a few minutes, I gathered enough strength to speak. "Get the fuck out of here."

She got up quietly, put on her clothes and left without saying a word.

Later that night, Pattie called. I hadn't seen her since the night we met at the Flamenco. She wanted to come over but she didn't know where I lived. I was definitely not in the mood for company. "You can come over tomorrow," I said.

"How do I get to your house?" she asked.

"Just call me from the Flamenco, and I'll have my driver pick you up," I replied.

Sure enough, the following night she called and I had Nelson pick her up. He returned with Pattie, beer, and a box of condoms, all delivered to my room. Rather than waste time with idle chit-chat, I got right to the point. "Take off your clothes."

Without hesitation, Pattie pulled her sweater over her head, kicked off her tennis shoes and peeled off the tight jeans. As I looked her over, I didn't even try to pretend she was there for any other purpose but to satisfy my sexual hunger.

"Lose the bra and panties," I said. Despite her large breasts, I could tell this girl was just a kid, no more than sixteen. "I'm gonna ask you a question and you tell me the truth. How old are you?"

"I told you, old enough," she said.

I had no patience for this. "Listen, I don't need any of your shit. Answer the fucking question and don't lie to me!"

She looked down at her feet. "Sixteen."

"Bullshit!" I shouted.

"Okay, okay. I'll be sixteen in a few months," she admitted.

"Fifteen years old," I said shaking my head. "You should be with your family. Put your fucking clothes back on. You're going home."

"I don't have a family," she said

"So where do you stay?" I asked.

"With friends," she answered.

I shook my head again, "So go back to your friends. I can't let you stay here."

"It's too late," she said. "If I'm not in by a certain time, they lock the doors."

I knew she was only telling half-truths. She was probably a runaway sleeping at a different house every night; exchanging sex for food and shelter. Give her a few months and she'd be working the streets with the pros. I felt sorry for her. "You hungry?"

"Yes," she said.

I got up. "Put your clothes on. Let's go upstairs and get you something to eat. You can stay tonight, but tomorrow you have to go."

She pulled her jeans on. "Please let me stay. I'll cook for you and take care of you."

"I already have a maid," I snapped.

"But I want to be your woman!" she insisted.

"Enough with that shit," I said, somewhat annoyed. "Hurry up and get dressed."

I took her upstairs to the kitchen and made her a couple of sandwiches. As she wolfed it down, I just sat there sipping my beer and looking at her. She didn't even notice me staring. When she was done, she washed it down with a beer and we went back to my room. I gave her a towel and showed her where the bathroom was. When she was done with her shower, she came into my room and climbed into bed. Without me saying a word, she started sucking on my nipples. In short order she was on top of me and we were having sex but I was too distracted to enjoy it. The whole time I just kept reminding myself that she wasn't my problem; that I wasn't the first to use her and I wouldn't be the last. Despite her pleading, I sent her on her way the following day.

Chapter 4
"The Performance"

Another two weeks passed. The neck brace came off and I was back at The Agency. It was good to be working again. My staff had missed me so much they decorated my office. There were cards and balloons, and even a cake. I didn't like all the fuss but it felt good to be missed. Within a week, everything was back to normal.

Then I got the phone call. It was Natasha announcing that she had something important to talk to me about that she couldn't tell me on the phone. I had a pretty good idea what it might be. Shit! How could I let this happen to me? "Okay, come over this Saturday," I said and hung up the phone.

When she came, I was sitting in the family room wearing shorts and a polo shirt. She was wearing a blouse and jeans. I had her sit next to me and offered her a beer. She took it and started sipping. I poured a shot of rum into a tumbler and gulped it down. Then I grabbed my beer and said gravely, "So what's on your mind?"

She was very nervous. "Xavier, I don't know how to tell you this. I'm so afraid."

"Natasha, how long have you known me?" I asked

"About two years," she replied.

"Right," I said, "and you know how I feel about our relationship and I'm sorry it's not what you want, but in all that time, have I ever given you bad advice?"

"No," she said.

I took her hands in mine. "And didn't I always say that as long as we were friends I would always be there for you?"

"Yes," she said.

I continued, "And who made it impossible to be friends because she wants more?"

A tear slid down one cheek, and was quickly followed by one on the other cheek. "I am," she admitted.

I gave her hands a gentle squeeze. "Natasha, I know it doesn't always look like it but I really care about you. I've always wanted the best for you and that's why we can't be together. But whatever it is, you can tell me."

I could see that my words were having an affect, but she wasn't ready to talk. This would take tact and patience, two things that I possessed in great abundance. I poured myself another shot, slugged it down, chased it with a mouthful of beer then got up still holding her hand, "Come on." I stamped out the cigarette I had left unattended in the ashtray and led her downstairs to my room.

As I stood behind her, I started to massage her neck and shoulders. My fingers searched out the little knots of tension and went to work on them. "Just relax, whatever it is, I promise it'll be all right." As I massaged, I started kissing her neck. I waited till I felt her shoulders relax, then I reached around to massage her breasts. She sighed and cocked her head back as I started on her nipples. Before she told me what she had to say, I had to find out for myself and there was only one way to do that. I started unbuttoning her blouse.

"Baby, I'm sorry we don't make love anymore," I said. "Heaven knows I want to. I still think about that day we spent at the Villa St. Louis."

I eased the blouse from her shoulders, tossed it onto the chair and turned her around to face me. Her cheeks were still wet but she had stopped crying. I pulled her to me and kissed her very softly and tenderly as I caressed her back. Every touch was calculated to make her feel that she was the only woman in the world who mattered to me.

With a deft move of one hand, I unsnapped her bra at the back, then pulled the straps forward and off her shoulders. She moved back a bit to allow me to remove the bra completely. Her breasts definitely seemed a bit fuller but that meant nothing. There was only one sure test.

I bent forward and took one of her nipples in my mouth. I swiped my tongue over it several times to remove any sweat and salt and swallowed my saliva. Ignoring her moans, I sucked on the nipple and focused everything on the taste. I hoped and prayed, and I sucked a little more. Once finished, I stopped, straitened and when I saw that she was looking at me, I gave her a warm smile and pulled her towards me in a hug so she wouldn't see my face. My heart was racing. This couldn't be happening but I knew it was. I knew exactly what she had come to say. Natasha was pregnant.

I weighed my options; maybe it wasn't mine. Very unlikely. I knew Natasha better than she knew herself. She wouldn't sleep with another man. So what else? There was only one choice. Abortion. Hopefully, she would make that decision herself. Otherwise, I would make that decision for her. Regardless, this fetus was as good as dead.

So I continued the charade, "Take off your jeans honey."

As she kicked off her tennis shoes and slipped out of her jeans, she was smiling at me with those adoring eyes. I eased her onto my bed then stepped back to admire her as I took my clothes off. I forced myself to go slow. I had to do everything in my power to promote the illusion that this would last forever. I pulled the polo shirt over my head. I smiled at her as I slowly dropped my shorts. When I was down to my briefs, I approached the bed and started kissing her. I kissed around her breasts, avoiding her nipples. I raised her arm up over her head and kissed a path down the side of her body from just above her ribs, down to her hip, then I traced the edge of her panties with my tongue. I kissed my way to her navel, pushed my tongue in all the way and kept pushing.

That caused her to finally break her silence. "Oh baby, I want you now, please."

I was tempted, but I couldn't risk it. Using just my touch, I had to convince her I loved her. I had to be patient. I left her navel and went to the leg band of her panties and started alternately kissing and licking my way all the way down to her ankles, taking extra time at her knees. When her body started to twitch at the slightest touch, I knew she was ready.

I stood up and slowly removed my briefs. I paused just a moment to let her see my erection, then turned and reached up to get a pack of condoms I had on a shelf above my desk. Since the shelf was above eye level, I took my time feeling around for the condoms. I turned around and as I walked towards her, I opened a condom and slowly unrolled it down the length of my penis. From the look in her eyes, there was no doubt that she was ready.

I climbed slowly onto the bed and took a position between her legs. I slipped my fingers under the waistband of her panties and on cue, she pushed her hips up off the bed. I pulled the panties towards me kissing her thighs and generally following the panties down her legs with my kisses. She raised her knees to her chest so I could remove the panties completely. When she lowered and spread her legs, I inserted only the head of my penis inside her. I darted in and out, then at random pulled out and rubbed the head against her clit, only to start the darting motion again. I wanted her wild with desire.

When I felt that she was near orgasm, I pulled out and started rubbing her clit with the head of my penis as I clamped my mouth on hers. She sucked my tongue greedily as she bucked under me and when she could no longer hold out, she turned her head to the side and made a soft weeping sound as she climaxed. As her orgasm was ending I inserted the full length of my penis inside her.

Startled, she said "Oh my god!" She grabbed my ass with both hands to pull me in as deeply as possible. I held it there motionless until I was sure her orgasm had completely passed. When her body finally stopped trembling beneath me, I started to kiss her face, neck and shoulders and began a slow grind with my hips. I stopped kissing her to look in her eyes. As we made contact, she smiled and tears started streaming down both sides of her face. Without missing a beat, I wiped her tears with my kisses, and as she closed her eyes, I placed a soft kiss on each eyelid, all the while building momentum in my hips. I started kissing her neck and shoulders again and waited. I didn't have to wait long.

Soon Natasha was moaning and grinding along with me. Gradually I went from grinding to pumping. A few minutes later, we both came together. Coming at the same time was the hardest part, but it was crucial. I had to make her believe there was a connection between us. We lay there, both of us spent. She, from two orgasms, and I, from my effort at self-control. I fully expected to be hearing from the Oscar nominating committee in the near future, but my performance wasn't over yet.

As I lay on top of her, I propped myself up on my elbows to leave space between her chest and mine. We were both covered in sweat and I started to blow on her face, neck and chest to cool her off. She let out a surprised gasp and opened her ever-adoring eyes to look up at me. I continued blowing on her, which allowed me to avoid her gaze. Eventually, she closed her eyes again. When her chest was cool, I rolled over onto my back. She rolled onto her side, put her head on my chest and draped one of her legs across mine. It was time to make my move. "Baby, go ahead and tell me what's wrong. No matter what it is, I'm here for you."

She let out a sigh, "I know, I didn't mean to doubt you. But it's just so hard."

"Take your time baby, take your time," I said as I caressed her head.

"Xavier... I wasn't feeling good..." She froze.

"Go on," I coaxed.

She took a deep breath, "I missed my period so I went to the doctor."

"What did he say?" I asked.

It took all her strength to speak the words: "Xavier... I'm pregnant."

I could feel the tears on my chest. "And what about you, how are you feeling? Are you okay?" I asked

"I guess so," she answered. "Xavier, I'm so sorry, I didn't mean..."

I interrupted her. "Hush, you don't need to apologize. We'll get through this."

"Oh baby," she started, "I was so scared. I was so sure you would hate me."

Little did she know how much I truly did hate her, but that wasn't the time, I had to stay cool. "Who else have you told?"

"No one else," she answered, "just my aunt."

That might be a problem. "Your aunt?" I asked. "How old is she?"

"She's twenty-five, but she's cool." Natasha answered. "She's the only person who knows all about us."

"Really," I said. "And what does she say about me?" This might be a big problem.

Natasha hesitated. "She says you are trying to protect me from your ex-wife and that's why you broke up with me."

I couldn't believe my incredible luck. This was perfect. "Sounds like your aunt really cares about you."

Natasha replied, "She does, she's my best friend in the world,"

After a short pause, I decided it was time. "Well, what do you want to do?"

"What do you mean?" she asked.

"What do you want to do about the pregnancy?" I said calmly.

"I want to keep the baby," she said, then paused. "Of course I want to keep the baby." Another pause. "Don't you want me to keep the baby?"

I reached over to the nightstand with my free hand, grabbed a cigarette and lit it. "Honey," I said softly, "I want you to listen very carefully." I took a long drag of the cigarette. "Whatever you decide, I'll support you because only you can make the best decision. And if your decision is to keep it, I'll do my part, but I'll only provide for the baby, do you understand?"

"No, I don't," came the worried reply. "What are you saying?"

"I'm saying what I've always said." I paused for effect. "You and I can be the best of friends but we can never be together. This pregnancy doesn't change that. As the father, I'm half responsible so I'll cover half the cost for pre-natal, hospital and all that. Your family will have to cover your half. And after the child is born I'll send you money every month, but that money will be for the child. I won't be able to support you. Not because I don't want to, but because I'm really not in a position to do it. Besides, I'll be moving back to New York later this year."

After a long pause Natasha said, "You're moving away? I didn't know that." Another long pause, "I understand, but I still want to keep our baby."

Not the answer I wanted, but I was ready. "Natasha, I know you want to keep it, but think of your future. Don't you realize that if you keep it you can kiss your medical career goodbye? All your dreams... gone. Everything you ever wanted out of life... lost forever."

I felt more tears on my chest and she was sniffing. "I don't want to lose our baby. If I can't have you, the baby will be like the next best thing. I don't want to give that up."

I reached over to the nightstand, pulled a handkerchief from the drawer and handed it to her. "I know sweetheart, it's a hard decision." I continued caressing her head. "But what will your family think? Your poor mother will be so disappointed if she finds out you're pregnant. And your brother, Jonah, he's worked so hard to provide for you since your father passed away. Is this any way to repay him? Whatever you decide, I'll support you 100%, but please, don't throw your life away. That would break my heart."

I had said enough. Now it was just a matter of waiting for my words to sink in, so I continued caressing her head as she cried.

Soon she was sobbing, but I still didn't say a word, I just let her get it out of her system.

"Xavier," she started, "I'm so afraid to do this. What if something happens to me? What if I die?"

I reassured her, "You won't die honey; I won't let anything happen to you. I know a very good doctor. He's the best. He'll take very good care of you."

She continued to sob for a few minutes without saying a word, then finally, "Okay, I'll do it," followed by a long silence.

Not good enough. I wanted to hear her say it. "What will you do?" I asked softly.

She didn't answer right away, she was still crying. Then, "I'll give up the baby."

Close enough, I could live with that answer. "Honey, I know this is the hardest decision you've ever made, but you'll see that it's really for the best."

"Xavier," she asked, "you'll be there with me right?"

There was no way in hell I would be seen anywhere near an abortion clinic with this girl. "Honey, I would love to be there with you but that's not a good idea. You should have a woman with you, someone like your aunt. Do you think she'll do that for you?" Everything rested on this one point.

Natasha answered, "I'm sure she will."

I wanted to let out a sigh of relief but her head was still on my chest. Now for the logistics: "Honey, before you go I'll give you some money and the address of a doctor not too far from your house. Like I said, he's very good. Make sure you tell your aunt everything I told you, okay?"

"Yes," she answered, "I will."

Later in the afternoon, I had the maid bring us dinner in my room. When night fell, I told Natasha she should go before her family got worried. I wrote the name and address of the doctor on a piece of paper and handed it to her along with $350; enough for the procedure and any meds the doctor would prescribe. I gave her a final hug and had Nelson drive her to the main road so she could catch a bus home.

The next few days were nail-biters. What if she changed her mind? What if getting her aunt involved back-fired? The only way I got sleep was to drink myself into oblivion every night and to make it through the work day I had to have three or four beers at lunch just to settle my nerves. I was in a bad state. But during the week

Natasha got the abortion. She had actually changed her mind, but her aunt convinced her that the abortion was for the best and went to the clinic with her. My instinct had served me well.

About a week after it was over, Natasha came to see me. I wanted to be absolutely sure she had really had the abortion. It was a Saturday and Nelson was out running errands with Pop. Mary bought her to my room.

"So, how did it go?" I asked.

"It hurts. I'm still sore," she answered. "The doctor told me that's normal. He gave me medicine for the pain along with antibiotics."

"Did you have enough money for all the meds?" I asked.

"Yes," she answered, "more than enough. Thank you. Thank you for everything. My aunt thinks you're a very special guy to take responsibility like this."

I really didn't want to hear this crap, but she kept talking. I tried to block it out but some words still made it through my alcohol-induced fog: Always love you... grateful... wonderful... happy together... thinking of you... and more. The more nice things she said, the more I hated her. How could anyone be this much in love?

I wanted her dead and I could think of no better way to kill her than to fuck her to death. I was drunk on rum, rage and hate. Without saying a word, I started undressing her. She wasn't sure what was going on but she did nothing to stop me. After I had her blouse unbuttoned, I said, "Take off your clothes."

Nervously, she stripped. "Baby, I want you too but I'm sore. The doctor said to wait a few weeks before having sex."

"I can't wait that long," I said harshly.

She said, "Okay, but go slow. Okay baby?"

I didn't answer. As I took off my clothes and put on a condom, she lay in bed and prepared to give herself to me.

"Get up!" I said.

She looked confused.

"Get up!" I shouted. "I want it from the back."

Even as she was getting up she was slowly shaking her head, "It's gonna hurt more that way."

"That's how I want it," I replied.

She got up, I turned her and bent her forward onto the bed. I grabbed her hip with one hand and guided my shaft with the other. Once my head was inside she let out a cry but I ignored her. I grabbed her by both hips and I pushed hard. Even as she cried out in pain, she accepted it. Her love for me was that great. The fact that she didn't struggle made me hate her that much more and I slammed into her again with more force. My hate for her was that blind. I pulled out and slammed into her again with an animal-like grunt. At this point she was sobbing. I pounded her another dozen times before I came. It was over quickly. I felt no pleasure at all, just a sinking feeling as I fell into the abyss of total moral depravity. I pulled out, removed the condom and wrapped it in tissue. As I did, I noticed it was tinged with red. I tossed it in the waste basket, put on my robe and went into the bathroom. As I showered, I did everything I could to block what I had just done out of my mind, but that was impossible.

When I went back in my room, Natasha was laying on her side, still naked, with her back to the door. In a weak voice she said, "It hurts Xavier."

"Get dressed," I said roughly.

She turned to look at me. "Xavier, it really hurts."

I looked in her eyes and glared with all the hate in my heart. "Get up! Get dressed! Get the fuck out of here!"

She was in a state of total shock. In that moment, she saw me as I truly was. The mask was off and my eyes were fixed on hers, giving her a full view of my soul, or lack thereof. She got up slowly, painfully, and put on her clothes as I stood and watched. When she was done, I stepped aside and pointed to the door. She stepped forward, stood for a moment and looked at me. For the first time I saw something in her eyes that I had never seen before: anger. Then she picked up her bag and walked past me. I followed her down the hall, out the door, through the lower courtyard, and down the path to the front gate. As she approached the gate, I passed her to open it and said, "Don't come back and don't call, ever!"

She looked at me. There were no tears, just the shell-shocked look of someone who has survived a disaster. "Why Xavier? I just want to know why."

"It's too late to talk about this," I said, "just go."

"Fine," she said, "fine." And as she stepped out the gate, "You'll pay for this Xavier. I swear to God you will pay."

Without even waiting for her to finish I closed the gate, locked it and went back to my room.

I wanted to be alone, but the voice inside my head wouldn't leave me: "Murderer! You killed the child and if given the chance you would kill the mother! Murderer!"

I had to get away from the voice. I knew I couldn't make it stop but I just wanted to get away from it. I didn't want to live with that voice even another minute or I would go crazy. "Murderer!"

I had something that might work, it was my only hope. There wasn't enough rum in the world, I needed something stronger. "Murderer!"

I climbed onto my chair, reached into the space above the book-case and pulled out a small piece of aluminum foil. I opened my desk drawer and pulled out a small pocket knife and a clear plastic tube. "Murderer!"

Carefully I unfolded the small square of foil and exposed the black resin. The pungent smell of opium-laced hashish filled the room. I scraped a small amount with the blackened tip of the knife. "Murderer!"

I put the tube to my mouth and used it to suck in the wisp of smoke that resulted from heating the tip of the knife. The effect was immediate. "Murderer." But I needed more. I needed to get as far from the voice as possible, so I took another hit and the voice became a faint whisper. I dropped everything into a drawer and collapsed into bed. I did my best to conjure up nice hallucinations, but the nice ones didn't want to have anything to do with me, so I wrestled with my demons until I eventually passed out.

Chapter 5
"Alice's World"

During the weeks that followed, I tried to fill my time as much as possible. A typical day meant getting to work thirty minutes late, working into the early evening (long after everyone else was gone), going straight from work to the Flamenco for dinner and drinks, then going home at around two o'clock in the morning.

Eventually, I got Bryan's version of what happened the night he trashed the Flamenco. According to him, we ironed out our differences over my bringing Anne-Marie into the restaurant and we spent the rest of the night drinking and talking. At some point, I got the bright idea of climbing up on the bar, but my hands slipped and I fell head first behind it, knocking myself out. Next, Bryan said he carried me to the spare bedroom and lay me on the bed, then went to sleep in his room. As much as I wanted to believe him, there were several things about his story that made no sense. Nonetheless, I kept my thoughts to myself and to this day, his story remains the official version of what happened. I reasoned that as long as Bryan and Anne-Marie were back together, that was all that mattered.

I did everything I could to forget Natasha, including spending more time with Pattie. I was taking her home with me more often. I even started noticing things about her, like her sense of humor. She was always making me laugh and I needed that, but I knew I had to end it. I also knew it was just a matter of time before Alice went after her.

But my main priority was work. I loved my job and I loved my staff. Olivia was the first addition to my team. I really resented her when she first started working for me. I had asked for a technical assistant and they had given me a secretary. Nonetheless, she managed to impress me by being a fast learner and thoroughly dedicated worker.

Leonard came on board as my senior technician about a year after Olivia. Always reliable and professional, he was an excellent technician. A year after that, I hired Leonard's friend, Ralph, as a full-time programmer.

When I started in 1991, I was twenty-six years old, engaged to Alice and my future looked fairly bright. With time, my responsibilities grew, along with my salary and my drinking. It had been about a year since I finally left Alice and my drinking and carousing were spiraling out of control.

Just down the street from the office, there was a small shopping center with exclusive shops and a little bistro. I would walk there for lunch everyday. Over time, I developed a rating system based on how many beers I had with lunch. If I had one beer, it was a normal day. If I was particularly happy or otherwise having a good day, I would celebrate by having two beers. Now if I was having a bad day, I would have at least three beers. The logic was that beer was a comfort food.

One day I was having an especially bad day. I went to the bistro, but I didn't crave anything on the menu. "No food today," I told the waiter, "just bring me a beer." My neck was really bothering me and even after four beers, I still felt irritable. I decided I was working too hard and needed a break. When I got back to the office, I called the dispatcher and told him I would be leaving at four o'clock. Jean was surprised because he always kept a driver late to take me home. I still wasn't driving because of the accident. Every morning, Jean sent a driver to pick me up at home, and every evening, a driver had to wait until I was done, and take me either home, or more likely, drop me off at the Flamenco. I was the only employee in the entire organization to be chauffeured this way and it cost The Agency significant money in overtime paid to the drivers, but Tony, my boss, approved it all. More than once I had a driver wait for me outside the Flamenco and I completely forgot about them once I started drinking. After a few hours they would call me on my two-way radio to ask if I was okay.

That day, when the driver dropped me off at my house, everyone was surprised to see me home so early. Nelson opened the gate. "Mr. Pouchon," he asked, "are you okay?"

I reassured him, "I'm fine Nelson, but I'm going out tonight. Not to worry, I'll drive myself."

The look on Nelson's face told me he was very worried. "I don't think that's a good idea, sir."

Good old Nelson, I didn't have a clue how much my stepfather was paying him, but he was priceless. I reassured him, "My neck is fine, there won't be any traffic, and I'll go early so I can park close to the entrance."

He protested as a matter of principal, but he knew it was pointless. Once I made up my mind that was pretty much the end of any debate. I went inside, up to the kitchen and got a beer out of the fridge. Nelson had told Mary I was home so she rushed upstairs to fix me dinner. It was early and I still wasn't hungry so I had her prepare just a small plate.

For a change, I asked to be served outside, in the upper courtyard. It was a secluded garden with fichus bushes, eucalyptus plants and several types of evergreen. The centerpiece was a pair of pine trees that grew straight up out of the ground and twenty feet into the air. For all their height, this particular species of pine had a trunk about a foot in diameter, and branches that spread out no more than two feet from the trunk. The upper courtyard was about twelve feet higher than the lower courtyard. A red metal gate opened onto the narrow stairs that connected the two courtyards.

The upper courtyard was designed to be an intimate, open-air retreat, while the lower was where the household staff lived and worked. A complex of rooms, built up around the lower yard provided living quarters for servants, storage, and a large kitchen. All these rooms were built on a 60,000 gallon water cistern that provided water to the large house. From the upper courtyard, one could see the bay of Port-au-Prince, and to the North, the massive mountain chain that went all the way to the northern part of the country. From the roof, the view was even more spectacular.

Mary set the table and I started to eat. Towards the end of my meal, Pop appeared in his robe and slippers. "You're home early," he said.

As he approached, I got up from the table, wiped my mouth and kissed him on the cheek. "Yes I am, I decided to take it easy today." I sat back down. "Sorry I didn't come greet you when I came in. I assumed you were sleeping."

"I was sleeping," he said with a smile. "You look fresh, going out tonight?"

"Yes, I'm going out, but I feel like crap. I'll take a nap after I eat, then I'll be fresh."

Despite his many weaknesses, I loved my stepfather. He was a kind and gentle man who loved to drink, laugh and talk politics. But more than anything else, he loved my mother and to him that meant loving my mother's kids more than his own. My mother had moved to New Jersey two years before, supposedly to support my sister in her studies at Marymount College. But I knew the real reason was Pop's drinking. The fact that Marymount was in New York, several hours away from my mother, pretty much confirmed my suspicions. Pop wasn't handling Mom's absence very well, but he never lost hope that she would come back. In the meantime, he dealt with it the only way he knew how, by drinking. He worked as the comptroller at a large factory and had a part-time job as the accountant at a commercial trade school.

"How was work today?" I asked.

"Work was good," he replied, "I'm not going to the school tonight so it's an easy day."

"When was the last time you went out? You should come with me," I offered.

"No way," he said, "you go and have fun. Besides, I'm working tomorrow." His answer wasn't surprising. When my mother left, Pop pretty much stopped going out. For him it just wasn't the same without her by his side.

Pop yelled for Mary but she didn't answer; she rarely did when it was him.

A few minutes later, Mary walked out into the courtyard, "Yes Mr. LeBaron."

"Bring me a glass of rum with some ice," Pop said in that gruff tone that seemed reserved for Mary.

"Mr. LeBaron, you won't get a drop of rum until you've eaten. You ready for dinner?"

"Just gimme some damn rum!" Pop demanded, "I'll eat after I've had a drink."

"Absolutely not," Mary countered, "not until you've eaten."

Pop looked at me with an exaggerated look of despair, "Do you see what I have to put up with?"

I couldn't help smiling and I turned to Mary, "Just bring him a little bit." Mary turned around and walked away. It didn't look like Pop was gonna get any rum. "You want me to get you a beer?" I offered.

Pop's eye lit up. "That's my boy!" Then he looked over his shoulder to make sure Mary wasn't eavesdropping. "You'll have to wait 'til she goes downstairs. If she catches you, she'll have a fit."

Mary was way ahead of us. She came back out with a platter and set a place in front of Pop. "Mr. Pouchon, you have to make sure he eats. You know what happens when he drinks on an empty stomach; he gets sick. Then who has to clean up after him? I do. And who has to take care of him? I do. It's not right…" Even as she walked away, she was still talking.

"You see," Pop said, "you see how she talks around me? No respect."

I smiled, leaned forward and kissed Pop on the forehead, "I know Pop, I know, just eat some of your food and save the rest for later. If you eat half, I'm sure Mary will give you some rum."

Getting Pop to eat was a constant fight. His liver was giving out and he couldn't keep any weight on, but he still wanted to drink like the old days. I loved Pop, but I could only see him this way for just so long before I had to go to my room.

As if on cue, Nelson came up the stairs from the lower courtyard. When he saw that I was done eating, he said, "I'll take care of him Mr. Pouchon." Then he turned to my stepfather and said, "Come on Pop, the sooner you eat, the sooner you get your rum."

I hated seeing Pop like that. I got up from the table, excused myself, thanked Nelson and went to my room. I needed to relax, but I was sick of rum, and beer wasn't strong enough. I needed to sleep for a couple of hours so I could go out that night. I knew exactly what would do the trick and it was still in the drawer where I had left it weeks before. My hands started to tremble as I pulled the drawer open. Sure enough, the small square of foil, the pocket knife and the plastic tube were still there. The image of Natasha's angry face flashed across my mind but even as her lips moved, it was Alice's voice that echoed inside my head, "You'll pay for this Xavier. I swear to God you will pay." The trembling got worse as I hurried to get high. I needed relief fast.

After taking a hit, I fell backwards onto the bed and started to imagine all the ways I would like to make love to Nadine, the receptionist at work. She looked so cute and sexy. But then, I saw Alice. Damn! She was looking good, but she wasn't alone. Who was that girl with her? It was Pattie. The two of them were French kissing, then they stopped and turned to look my way, inviting me to join them. Then I saw Natasha. She was crying and had something in her arms that she was trying to give me. It was wrapped in bloody cloth. I turned to get away, only to see a woman standing naked in the shower, holding onto the heavy metal bar. When I looked closer, I realized she was tied to the bar with the belt from my new robe. Her back was to me as water rained down on her from the ceiling, but I knew it was my cousin, Mickey, because of the ribbons in her hair. I turned to leave the bathroom but found myself face to face with Yasmine. She kept pushing me backwards until I felt my cousin's cold, lifeless body against my back. And so it continued, all the women in my life, going from one grotesque scene to another until I passed out.

Despite the hallucinations, I woke up several hours later feeling pretty good. I showered and dressed, then drove Pop's white Mazda 626 coupe to Pétion-Ville. Rather than go to the Flamenco, I decided to go to the Snack Shack for dinner. Not only did I want something different to eat, but I wanted to be alone. I knew if I went to the Flamenco Pattie would be there and I just wasn't in the mood for her company.

The Snack Shack had been around for years. Despite all the changes, it was still a favorite hangout for the young crowd. I started going there while I was still in high school. Ken, the Canadian owner, was a total dick. It wasn't so much how he treated his customers, but how he treated Pete, his son. When we were in high school, Pete caught his dad fucking his girlfriend! Ken even got the girl pregnant and married her. He long ago divorced her and just kept going through teenage girls like they were going out of style. Got most of them pregnant too. Ken was actually proud of all his kids but he was most proud of the fact he always had some beautiful dimwitted teenager on his arm. Over the years, he turned more and more of the restaurant over to Pete to the point where Pete pretty much ran the place. Not that Ken had much choice; most people hated him, but the more Pete did with the place, the more business picked up. Ken may have been a dick, but he wasn't stupid and he knew what was best for business.

I was sitting at an outside table enjoying my fried chicken basket when my ex-wife, Alice walked in the place. She was looking good, very good. From the mini-dress to the designer shoes and matching hand-bag, it was clear that fucking my friends was paying off handsomely. She looked around until she saw me, walked over and without invitation, sat at my table.

"Mind if I join you?" she said as she flashed her most seductive smile.

"You mean I have a choice?" I replied sarcastically.

She ignored my comment and lit up a cigarette. "So how you been?"

"Fine," I said without looking up from my meal.

"And your neck?" she persisted.

"Fine," I answered in my most monotone voice, hoping she'd get the hint, but knowing that wouldn't stop her.

"Oh, don't mind me honey," she offered, "you go right on eatin'."

"Alice, that's real nice of you," I said, every syllable dripping with sarcasm. "What do you want?"

She just turned up the charm, "Baby, I don't want nothin' from you. I jus' wanna help you. You know that's all I eva wanted ta do."

"What makes you think I need help?" I asked.

"Xavier, you really need to be careful who you hangin' aroun' wit."

I continued eating. "Whatever you say Alice."

"So where you find that lil hood-rat you been fuckin'?" she asked.

"I have no idea what or who you're talking about," I replied while munching on a drumstick.

"Sweetheart, you can't lie ta me," she said with that wicked smile of hers. "You know exactly who I'm talkin' 'bout."

A waiter walked up to the table and looking at Alice, asked, "Would you like to order anything?"

"No," I said, "she's about to leave."

Alice smiled at the waiter, "I'll have a glass of lemonade please, with extra sugar on the side," and then as he walked away she turned to me, "Xavier, why you gotta make it so hard? All I wanna do is protect you."

I just kept eating and with my eyes on my food and a mouth full of chicken, I said, "Ya don't say."

She ignored my sarcasm and kept right on going. "Darlin' you really should stay away from those street bitches. You know they only bring trouble."

I wanted so much to tell her off. In fact, I wanted to choke the shit out of her. I looked at her neck and imagined myself squeezing that scrawny little stick between her head and shoulders. Then as I imagined her eyes rolling back into her head, I said, "Alice, is it too much to ask to eat a meal in peace? I am paying for this, you know."

"Baby, I don't want no trouble." she said, "Okay, I'll go, but it's my duty to warn you not to trust that lil bitch Pattie. She'll turn on you. I spoke ta her the otha day, and she tol me everythin'. How you fucked her. Where you fucked her. What you had fa dinna. She even described everythin' in your room." Alice paused for extra effect and leaned forward. "When didja get da new robe Xavier?"

I stopped eating and looked up at her.

Satisfied with herself, she leaned back, took a long drag of her cigarette and said, "And ya really should tell that stepfatha a yours ta keep his hands ta himself, the drunken fool was all ova her. No wonda yo motha lef' his sorry ass."

Several times, I had come close to killing Alice. Several times, she had lain unconscious on our bed as I stood over her with a pillow. But I didn't do it. I chose to do the right thing, even though I had it all planned out: disposal of her body, an alibi and even a ticket out of the country. But in that moment I truly regretted not having killed her when I had the chance.

Alice put on an air of mock surprise, "Oh, I'm sorry. She didn't tell you? Why would she hide that from you, Xavier? I know it ain't outa shame. Lil ho woulda fucked 'im too if he wasn't too damn cheap ta pay her. Don't look surprised Xavier; ya know she's a fuckin' ho!"

I knew what she was saying about Pop wasn't true but I felt the fury building inside me. I also knew that the worst thing I could do was get upset, but she had pushed the last button. "Okay that's it, get the fuck outta here!"

Alice laughed and said, "Relax Xavier, no need ta git upset. Soon as my lemonade comes I'll leave you be." She stopped smiling and looked me dead in the eyes. "But jus' rememba, there ain't no place on earth you can go that I won't follow. You can go ta Africa, Europe, or back to the States, that won't keep me from findin' you.

Even if I have ta fuck every ambassador between here and China, I'll follow you, Xavier. I know you'll neva come back ta me, but if I can't have you, no one havin' you. 'Specially not some ten-dolla ho. So go 'head, fuck her while ya can, but I'll find her some night when you ain't aroun' and I'll take my time cuttin' her up. And while I'm doin it, I'll let her know you made me do it. I'll make sure she dies hatin' your fuckin' guts."

Right about then the waiter appeared with her lemonade.

Alice smiled at him and said, "Thank you sweetie," and as she got up from her chair, she took her lemonade and the extra packets of sugar. "Just put it on his bill." She then turned, smiled to me and said, "Bye Xavier, love you." And with that she blew me a kiss and walked to the bar.

I was furious. I wanted to get up but I realized I was shaking. No matter what, I had to stay in control. I just sat there for a minute, then took several deep breaths and called for the waiter. The waiter snapped around and several of the patrons turned towards me to see what the commotion was about. Alice was at the bar already flirting with one of the customers, but she still turned and smiled at me. I was so upset I didn't even realize I had yelled. The waiter rushed over and I asked for a double shot of Jack Daniels and the bill. As much as I hated Alice, what I wanted most at that moment was to slap the shit out of Pattie. That stupid bitch! All she had to do was keep her fucking mouth shut. Damn it! I'd take care of her in a bit, but first I had to settle my nerves. When the waiter came back, I gulped the double, paid him, and walked past Alice and out the gate.

The Flamenco was a short walk right around the corner. By the time the shots started to kick in, I was going down the stairs into the bar. I sat in my usual spot and without saying a word, Jacky put a beer in front of me. Something about the look on my face told her I didn't want to talk. Bryan came over and sat on the stool across from me. "What's up buddy?"

"Nothing much," I said.

"Dominos or dice?" Bryan asked.

"Dominos," I answered.

We played in silence until a few more regulars showed up, then we paired up and played two against two. It was a ritual established over hundreds of nights. Renaldo, a Mexican diplomat, was my partner that night. My focus was way off; I couldn't follow his lead to save my life. After losing four straight sets, I bought a round of drinks for the players and talked someone into taking my place.

I moved to a small table between the bar and the restaurant and had Jacky bring me another beer. As I sat drinking, Pattie walked in but I almost didn't recognize her. Her hair was permed and she was wearing a dress and heels. She was also wearing makeup that made her look five years older. When she saw me, she smiled, came straight to my chair, sat in my lap and kissed me on the mouth. "Hi baby. How was your day?"

"My day was shit!" I said in a gruff voice and pointed to the chair across from me. "Sit down!"

"What's wrong baby?" she asked.

I wasted no time. "I had one simple rule and you had to fucking break it. What did I tell you would happen if you talked to my ex-wife?"

"But baby…"

I cut her off. "No fucking buts. The rule was simple, the rule was for your protection, you broke the fucking rule, it's over. Lose my phone number and forget where I live."

Jacky came to the table and put a beer in front of Pattie.

"Jacky," I said, "Pattie will pay for her own drinks. Take her off my tab." I stood up, finished my beer, handed the empty bottle to Jacky and walked toward the stairs. "Good night fellas, see you tomorrow,"

The chorus of voices answered "good night" as I went up the stairs. Walking back to the car, I couldn't get Alice out of my mind. Even as I drove, I couldn't help recalling the many fights and arguments we'd had. I didn't want to think about her, but when I was home alone in my room with the adrenaline still flowing, there was little else to occupy my mind.

⋙:⋘

Two years earlier, life with Alice was becoming unbearable. I was getting tired of her insane jealousy and I finally decided that being a faithful husband was overrated and not worth the misery I was going through. It was about that time that I met Natasha but despite my initial advances, everything changed when I learned that she was only sixteen. I got sex off my mind and we became friends. I made no secret of the fact I was in an unhappy marriage, but rather than trouble her with my own problems, I became her confidant and counselor. I enjoyed our regular telephone conversations very much but Natasha was young and impressionable and things just got more complicated as she fell more deeply in love with me. For nine months, I restrained myself and resisted all her attempts to get more intimate. That was, until one day, after weeks of constant fighting with Alice, I made one of the biggest mistakes of my life.

Since I came home drunk every night, that made it relatively easy to tune her out, so Alice started calling me at work. She pushed every button until one day I slammed the phone onto the cradle and decided that I had had enough. I needed to get away so I left the office and drove to Natasha's house, hoping she was home from school. When I got there, she was both surprised and happy to see me. She was getting ready to go to volleyball practice but decided to spend some time with me instead, and asked if I would take her to another house her family owned a few miles out of town.

There was no traffic, it was a beautiful day, and the drive away from the hustle and bustle of the city was very relaxing. When we got to the property, there were two houses. Natasha explained that the larger house towards the front was where she spent weekends and most of her vacations. The smaller one in the rear was being rented out. Natasha let us in and after closing the door behind us, turned to look at me and smiled. In that moment, the constant strife with Alice seemed a world away. Natasha wrapped her arms around me and it was gone entirely.

I hesitated a moment before putting my arms around her. I knew there was something wrong with this situation but I was so aroused that I couldn't think clearly. Instead of kissing her, I leaned forward and sniffed her neck, thinking that would be safer, but Natasha's natural scent was a powerful aphrodisiac. Before I knew it, we were rubbing our bodies together and breathing heavily. After holding back for nine months, I knew that any further resistance was pointless. I kissed her on the lips and in an instant all her pent-up desires were released. We had passed the point of no return and suddenly everything seemed clear. I abandoned all my doubts as I began to undress her, then I realized we had a problem.

I shook free of her arms and took a step back. "Natasha! I don't have any condoms."

Her eyes widened. "Baby please don't say that."

"It's true," I replied. "I never keep any on me. What would I need them for?"

"Okay," she said. "There's a little store right around the corner. You can buy some there."

The store was more like a stand on the side of the road, but I remembered seeing it. "You sure they sell condoms?"

"Absolutely," she said, "you'll see them hanging on the wall behind the clerk."

It was all I needed to hear. I hurried off and when I got back, Natasha had stripped down to her bra and panties. I undressed as fast as I could and we made love like we had both been locked up for ten years and were going back to jail later that night.

When we were done, I looked at my watch. "Holy shit! We gotta get out of here." I jumped up and started putting my clothes on.

Natasha sat up in bed. "You go on. You'll get back to the office faster if you don't have to worry about me. I'll take the bus."

I leaned forward and gave her a quick kiss on the lips. "Thanks baby."

Natasha jumped up and put her arms around my neck. "At least you can give me a real kiss before you go."

Our lips locked and my hands were irresistibly drawn to the curves of her body. Before I knew it, I was pulling my clothes off and we were making love again.

When I finally got back to the office, it was past quitting time and the building was empty. I stayed late catching up on my paperwork and then went to the Flamenco for drinks.

Over the next three months, Natasha and I met like that five or six times. Suddenly, life with Alice wasn't so unbearable anymore. I just had to be careful and not get caught. Then one Saturday night after a particularly nasty fight I decided to spend a whole day with Natasha. The next morning I was up much earlier than usual for a Sunday and told Alice I'd be spending the day with my stepfather. She didn't like that, but there really wasn't much she could say about it. Also, it was the perfect alibi, since it would be almost impossible for her to check up on me. She and my parents were mortal enemies.

Natasha was very surprised when I showed up at her house. When I asked her if she wanted to spend the day with me, she reacted as though I had asked her to marry me. Her enthusiasm was a welcome contrast to Alice's constant bickering. I parked my motorcycle in her yard and we took a taxi to the Hotel Villa St. Louis.

The hotel seemed almost empty except for a small party of four sitting on the far side of the pool. Seeing her in a bikini, it was impossible to keep my hands off Natasha. There we were, in the perfect setting where I could shower her with affection and not worry about being seen. After lunch, I checked us into a room and we spent the rest of the day making love until well into the evening.

Everything changed that Sunday and it soon became obvious that Natasha had decided to do whatever was necessary to be with me. The next day I realized I had made a big mistake, but it would take a major incident to show the true magnitude of my lapse in judgment. Where Natasha used to be discreet, she had become careless. Despite my best efforts and strong warnings, she left a trail of clues that led Alice right to her house. It was the break Alice had been looking for. Insane with jealousy, she tried to storm Natasha's house and had to be subdued by two of Natasha's brothers. The entire time Alice was screaming obscenities and accusing Natasha of everything from adultery and prostitution to incest and bestiality. Drawn by all the drama, the entire neighborhood gathered in front of Natasha's house until the police finally came, broke it up and took Alice away.

At the police station, Alice used every trick of manipulation to convince the police that she was the victim. She even filed a police report accusing Natasha of assault and battery. According to the report, Natasha's brothers grabbed her as she happened to be walking past their house and held her while Natasha roughed her up.

All this happened while I was at work. When Natasha called, the only reason I had taken the call was to tell her it was best if we never saw each other again. Before I could say a word, she said hysterically. "Xavier, Alice is taking me to court!"

"What the hell are you talking about?" I asked in disbelief.

"They came to my house today with a police officer. If my family hadn't hidden me, they would have taken me to jail!" Natasha was in tears.

"You're not making any sense," I said. "Calm down and start from the beginning." I couldn't believe my ears as Natasha filled me in on all the events of the day. Both Alice and Natasha were being required to appear before the judge in a few days and Natasha's family wanted me dead. I knew immediately that there was only one way out, and that was to gamble everything. "Natasha, I want to speak to your family. Tell them I'll be there later today. All I ask is that they listen to me for five minutes. After that, they can do whatever they want."

When I got to her house, I was sure that I had made a terrible mistake when two of Natasha's brothers grabbed me. They were about to start pummeling when the oldest brother, Jonah, ordered them to hold off. Jonah, a forty-something looking man, was tall, rugged and looked like he could put a serious beating on anyone stupid enough to take him on. He glared at me. "You have five minutes before we make you pay for what you did to our sister, so start talking!"

My heart was racing. "Can we please go inside? I know when you hear what I have to say, you'll feel very differently about all this. And if I'm wrong… well, we know what happens if I'm wrong."

Jonah ordered the two younger men to release me and he led the way inside. The other two followed behind; escape was impossible. Natasha and her mother were both sitting on the couch. Natasha looked at me briefly and then looked down at the floor. Tears were streaming down her cheeks. Her mother looked at me and shook her head slowly as I entered the room. From the redness in her eyes, I could tell she had been crying as well. Jonah gestured to a chair in the corner of the small living room and I sat down uncomfortably as the three men stood blocking the doorway.

I cleared my throat and made eye contact with everyone in turn as I started: "First let me say that I take full responsibility for what happened today. I'm here to explain myself and tell you the whole story. I've known Natasha for a year and I can tell you that in all that time she has never done anything that would bring disrespect to herself or her family. Soon after we met, she told me she was sixteen and I told her I was married. For both of those reasons, I have never touched her." I paused a bit so my lie could have its full effect.

Natasha looked up at me with the saddest of expressions. It obviously hurt to hear me deny our relationship so completely. Fortunately, all eyes were on me so I continued. "Instead, she and I have become very close friends and I've done everything I could to help her and guide her. As you all could see today, my wife is a very sick woman. She is a cross I've had to bear for several years now. I'm absolutely miserable in my marriage, but because she is mentally ill, I have to care for her." Natasha's mother nodded approvingly. "I don't know how she found out about my friendship with Natasha, but I have to assume that all my precautions just weren't enough. In any case, I recognize that Natasha is just an innocent victim and I promise that you will never have to worry about my wife again."

I looked around the room and I was relieved to see that none of the faces looked as angry anymore. I let out a sigh before starting again. "I know that you have to appear in court. I'll be there and I'll take care of everything. All I ask is that no matter what my wife says, please ignore her and don't say anything. She will do everything in her power to get you to react, but just ignore her. If you ignore her, she will eventually start cursing and yelling like she did today and the judge will see that she is insane. When I'm asked to speak, I'll tell the judge that Natasha is innocent and my wife is mentally ill. That should be more than enough to have the case thrown out."

The brothers looked at each other and I paused long enough for them to turn towards me again. "But the most important reason why

I came here today is to tell you all in person how truly sorry I am. I love Natasha very much and never meant to hurt her." Natasha looked up at me and I could see a look of wonder in her eyes. Not once had I ever told her that I loved her, and this was the closest I would ever come. "I have no words to express how heartbroken I am about this whole incident. Thanks for listening to me, that's all I have to say." Less than five minutes and my speech was over. The younger men looked at Jonah, Jonah turned to his mother, and without saying a word, she nodded to him.

Jonah turned back to me. "You're a brave man coming here by yourself after all the trouble you've caused. When our father died I became the man of this family." He pointed to Natasha, while still looking at me. "Natasha is the baby so I watch over her very carefully. She's always been a pretty good kid and does as she's told, so I seldom have to discipline her. But today I gave her a beating she won't soon forget." Natasha looked down at the floor, clearly embarrassed and Jonah continued. "But it was nothing compared to what we were going to do to you."

I swallowed hard before looking him in the eyes. "I have a little sister too. I would do the same. She's very lucky to have brothers like you."

Jonah looked at Natasha, then back to me. "I can see why my sister likes you. Only a decent man would come to us the way you did today. After what happened earlier, I told my sister she was never to talk to you or see you ever again." Jonah looked at his mother and she nodded again. "Take care of this situation with the judge and you have my blessing to see my sister. You just have to promise to keep your crazy wife away from her. I'm really sorry about your marriage."

Holy shit! What the hell kind of mess had I gotten myself into and what the fuck did he mean by "blessing?" My mind was swimming as I scrambled to find the right words. "I don't know what to say... I mean of course I'll make sure your sister is safe."

"And you promise to take care of the judge?" Jonah asked.

"Absolutely!" I answered. "If you don't say a word and let me do all the talking, I promise the judge will dismiss the case and this will all be behind us."

Jonah stepped towards me with a slight smile and extended his hand. I stood and gave him a firm handshake. The other two brothers came in turn and each shook my hand. Natasha stayed in her seat but her mother stood. I approached her and gave her a hug. As I did, she smiled and spoke for the first time. "Go in peace, my son."

I looked at Natasha and nodded to her. I knew it would be most inappropriate to touch her in any way. She smiled discreetly and looked down at the floor, and then Jonah walked me back to my motorcycle.

That night when I got home, Alice was scantily dressed and had a nice dinner waiting for me, but I wasn't interested. I confronted her immediately and within seconds, we were shouting at each other. Of course she accused me of cheating with Natasha, and of course, I denied it. Before I knew it, she drew a knife. I grabbed her wrists and we wrestled around the house, breaking everything in our path as we went along. When I finally got the knife out of her hand, I was furious. I grabbed her by the throat and started squeezing. She fought with all her might but at barely a hundred pounds, she didn't stand a chance. I really don't know what made me finally stop squeezing, but when I did, Alice started gasping for air. I stood up and stepped away from her. Alice crawled a few feet in my direction as she fought to catch her breath.

When she could finally speak, she looked up at me. "You were gonna kill me for your little whore?" I shook my head but she kept talking. "You'll pay for this Xavier. I swear to God you will pay."

I turned around and left the house. That night I slept at the Flamenco. I went back home the next day but Alice and I didn't say a word to each other.

The day of the hearing, I left the house at my usual time, but I didn't go to work. I called the office and told them I had an emergency; then I drove to Natasha's. I wanted to see her family before they went to court. I stayed outside with the brothers to reassure them everything would be fine and reminded them to ignore anything Alice said. I didn't get to see Natasha but that was just as well.

From there I went for a ride to clear my head. I considered breakfast but I couldn't eat. Finally, I went to the Flamenco. It was closed, but Max let me in and Roland offered me a drink. After two drinks, it was time to go. I got to the courthouse thirty minutes early. I wanted to make sure I was the first one there. After waiting a bit, Natasha and her family appeared. I approached them discreetly and explained that it wouldn't be wise for the judge or any of the court officers to see me talking to them. Besides, if asked, I intended to tell the judge I barely knew Natasha and I had never met any of the other members of her family.

They were all nervous, even Jonah, and Natasha was shaking visibly. I was scared too but I knew they were counting on me so I put on an expression of absolute confidence and smiled at them. "Don't worry, let me do all the talking and everything will be fine. I promise." Then I nodded, turned and went inside the courtroom.

The single courtroom had a dozen or so benches. I sat in the far back corner so I could see everyone as they entered. A few minutes later, I heard loud voices out in the hallway. One of them belonged to Alice. The door opened and she entered. Even as she made her way to the far end of the first bench, she was hurtling insults out the open door. Natasha's family entered angrily. Damn, the proceedings hadn't even started yet and she had succeeded in getting them upset enough to argue with her. It was bad, very bad. I stood up and caught Jonah's eyes. I frowned at him and shook my head slowly from side to side. He let out a sigh and shushed his family before corralling them at the opposite end of the front bench.

Alice turned and saw me sitting in the back. Without even trying to hide her anger, she got up and walked up to me. "What the fuck are you doing here?"

My heart was beating somewhere up near my throat, but I kept a cool appearance and smiled. "As your husband, I'm required to be here."

"Why," she snapped back, loud enough so the whole room could hear, "so you can defend your little whore?"

"No," I replied calmly, "because it's the law."

Right about then a police officer entered the room. "Order in the court! All rise for the honorable Judge Mondesir."

Everyone stood and I followed Alice back to the first row of benches and stood next to her. Once the courtroom was still, a pretty, forty-something woman in a long black robe entered the room, walked up to the dais, sat in the over-stuffed chair and pounded her gavel one time. "You may all be seated." The judge took a few minutes to review the file.

A female judge! I couldn't believe my luck. Even if Alice didn't have an outburst, it was very unlikely this would go very far. Alice was here alone, representing herself, while Natasha was here with her family, and basically, looked like an innocent school-girl.

The judge signaled to the court officer and whispered in his ear. He then stepped forward and read from the file. "Judge Mondesir will now hear the case of Pierre versus Joseph. Alice Pierre please approach the bench."

Alice walked up to the dais and started talking, "Judge, I demand justice! That woman and her family," Alice pointed to Natasha, "attacked me without provocation…"

The Judge pounded the dais with her gavel. "Hold on Mrs.

Pierre, you'll get your chance, but this is a hearing, not a trial. I'm here to determine whether or not a crime has been committed, and whether a trial is necessary. Please keep your statement brief and stick to the facts. Now start by stating your full name and address for the record."

Alice took a deep breath to calm herself then spoke her name. The proceedings went pretty much as I had predicted. After Alice finished with her fantastic story of being kidnapped, tortured and beaten, Natasha was asked to approach the bench and not only refuted everything Alice had said, but added that she had never met Alice until the day of the incident. Furthermore, she said that even then she only saw Alice through a window, because her mother kept her in the house as Alice tried to fight two of her brothers in the front yard.

Several times, Alice tried to provoke Natasha and her family but they simply ignored her. This infuriated Alice and the outbursts occurred with increasing frequency. Judge Mondesir was not amused and several times threatened to hold Alice in contempt. Eventually, I was asked to approach the bench. I told the judge Alice was emotionally disturbed, that I had no idea why she had chosen these innocent people as her latest target and I wanted to extend my sincerest apologies to the honorable judge for wasting so much of the court's precious time with my poor wife's delusional behavior. Alice went berserk. She lunged towards me and tried to tackle me to the ground, all the while screaming obscenities at the top of her lungs. When the court officer tried to subdue her, she scratched his arm and tried to bite him. Judge Mondesir ordered the case dismissed and a second officer was called in to restrain Alice.

∽:∾

Two nights later, I drove back up to Pétion-Ville. It was Thursday and Freddy's band would be at the Flamenco. When I got there, it was busy and I had to find a parking space down the street. I was barely out of the car when a little boy, no more than seven ran up to me. "Mr. Xavier, I'll watch your car!" But no sooner had he said those words when a bigger boy, maybe twelve years old, pushed him aside. "Don't listen to him Mr. Xavier. He's too small; I'll watch your car. Both boys were filthy. The older boy wore a dirty rag that may have once been a red t-shirt. His pants were several sizes too big and made of very thin material. A piece of rope served as a belt. The younger boy had no shirt at all and wore a dirty pair of jeans. Both boys were barefoot. The younger boy picked himself up and charged the older boy.

"Hey! Stop that!" I yelled. Both boys turned to look at me. I leaned against my car, as I looked the two boys over, letting the silence speak for me. They were both looking down at the ground with their hands behind their backs. "How many times do I have to tell you two?" Both boys started to squirm and fidget. I looked at the older boy, "John, didn't I tell you that you are to watch over your little brother no matter what?"

"Yes Mr. Xavier," the older boy answered.

Then I turned to the younger one, "Timmy, what did you do to piss John off?" Both boys started speaking at once. "Enough!" I yelled. "You can both watch my car." Normally, each boy would get a dollar, but the smallest bill in my wallet was a five. I gave the money to the older boy and made him promise to give the younger boy $2.50 as soon as he made change. By then a group of a dozen or more street kids had gathered around us, all offering to watch my car. "Sorry boys, these two were here first." And I made my way to the restaurant.

John and Tim were not actually brothers, but they were insepa-rable. Like most of the other boys, they were homeless. I always made time to talk to these street kids and tried to teach them the importance of sticking together.

When I got inside, the place was packed and I saw Pattie sitting near my usual spot. She had her back to me and was talking to a man who looked about fifty. I walked right past her into the restaurant and hoped she hadn't seen me. Freddy and his band were doing sound checks and the show was about to start. I stopped Paul, one of the waiters, and asked for a table as far away from the music as possible. He led me to a small table in the far corner of the garden. I looked up at the clear sky. This was perfect. No one would find me here unless they came looking for me. I almost never sat out here, so I was sure I would have some privacy.

As I sat down, I gave Paul my order. "Pepper steak medium rare, baked potato heavy sour cream, a side of angel hair pasta with herb sauce, extra garlic rolls, and start me off with some fried mozzarella sticks and a glass of red wine." I knew the menu by heart; in fact, I had done the typesetting as a favor to Bryan and Roland.

Paul brought me my wine just as the band started to play. Freddy was pretty good and he got the crowd excited. I was able to enjoy my meal in complete privacy and Paul made sure my wine glass was always full.

Soon after my meal, Pattie made her way to my table. Not surprisingly, someone had tipped her off that I was in the garden. She was wearing a mini-skirt and a tight top with a plunging V-neck that highlighted her breasts and some nice heels that she obviously wasn't too comfortable in. Her hair was styled fashionably and her make-up was very well done. She even had a gold chain around her neck and gold hoops hanging from her ears to round out the package. It was impossible to tell that Pattie was only fifteen.

"Xavier, can I talk to you please?" she said timidly.

I didn't say a word; I just nodded to the chair across from me.

As she sat down, she started, "Xavier, I know you're mad at me but I want to explain."

"There's nothing to explain," I interrupted.

"Xavier please," she begged, "please give me another chance."

"Pattie, you had your chance," I reminded. "You proved that I can't trust you."

Pattie looked desperate. "Xavier, Alice told me all about you, and I don't care. I still love you."

Alice was a master of manipulation and deceit. Her secret was that every single lie she told was wrapped around an item of truth. Alice knew every skeleton in my closet by name and Pattie was completely under her spell.

I was calm, but I wasn't gonna argue all night. "So tell me Pattie, did she tell you these things about me before or after you described my room to her?" Pattie was stunned but I continued. "I told you to stay away from her, and that was for your own protection."

"You're wrong Xavier!" Pattie shot back, "she would never hurt me."

A bit surprised, I leaned back in my chair and considered the possibilities. "Where have you been getting money for the clothes, the hair and all the rest?" Pattie looked down at her hands and didn't say a word. I leaned forward and grabbed her roughly by the wrists. "I asked you a fucking question!"

Without looking up Pattie answered, "When I met Alice the other day I remembered what you told me, but she was nothing like that. She bought me dinner and we talked. I didn't mean to say anything wrong, but she already knew everything anyway. After that, she asked me where I was staying and I told her I didn't know, so she offered to let me stay with her. She lets me wear her clothes."

I had to laugh. Even after all these years, Alice still had new tricks up her sleeve. When she had been threatening to cut Pattie that was all a sham. She had already made Pattie her bitch. And from the looks of it, she was taking pretty good care of her. I let go of Pattie's wrists, "Go back to Alice. She wouldn't want you talking to me."

"But she gave me permission," Pattie said.

"Permission for what," I asked, "to talk to me?"

Pattie looked up at me, "Permission to sleep with you." And after a short pause, "Please Xavier, just one last time. We can go to a hotel, I have money."

In a sudden fit of rage, I leaned forward and growled in her face, "Fuck you, bitch! And you tell that fucking cunt ex-wife of mine…" but I caught myself. This was exactly what Alice wanted. Breathing heavily, I sat back in my chair. "Just get the fuck away from me."

Pattie started crying but she didn't say another word as she got up and walked away.

That pretty much ruined my night, so after another drink I left the Flamenco and went home.

Chapter 6
"Fresh Meat"

About two weeks later, I had a driver from the office drop me off at the Flamenco and I sent him on his way. It was Friday afternoon and I wanted to go barhopping. Since it was early, I had a few beers with Bryan and then told him I would see him later. There was a certain feeling in the air. It was almost electric. All the bars were packed with young people out to have a good time, American military, and American contractors attached to the US military presence in Haïti. Business was booming for the restaurant and bar owners of Pétion-Ville. After having a few drinks at most of the better bars on the one-way street that led through the heart of downtown Pétion-Ville, it was time to go back to the Flamenco. By then, it was well into the night and only the serious party people would be there.

From the looks of the cars outside, I could tell it was hopping at the Flamenco. I was on the prowl for fresh meat and I had a feeling I would score big that night. As I got to the bottom of the stairs, I checked out the crowd at the bar. It was packed. A few regulars, lots of marines looking to get lucky and lots of young women looking to land a big fish. Most of the girls looked familiar, but one girl stood out because I had never seen her before.

She was about five feet two and slim, maybe a hundred pounds, dark skin, short hair, and a pretty face. She wore a pair of denim shorts, a large white t-shirt with a bright tropical design and the words 'Kaliko Beach Club' in large letters across her chest, and beach sandals that flattered her delicate ankles and pretty toes. Sitting next to her was a young man in his early twenties, wearing khaki shorts, a camouflage print t-shirt and flip-flops. From his crew cut hair, I could tell he was a marine. The two of them were talking and laughing so it was obvious they were together.

I decided right then and there that I had to have this girl. I stood far enough away so as not to be noticed, got Jacky's attention and signaled her to get me a beer. With my beer in hand, I planned my strategy. First, I would have to get rid of the boyfriend. Patiently I waited for my opportunity. I didn't have to wait long before the girl got up to go to the bathroom. I quickly finished my beer and walked up to the newly vacant stool.

Predictably, the marine started the conversation, "I'm sorry, this seat is taken."

"Oh, I know," I replied, "I just want to get the waitress's attention and I'll be out of your way. My name's Xavier."

He reached out to accept my hand and introduced himself with a thick southern accent. "My name is Joey."

"So Joey, where are you from?" I asked with a smile.

Joey smiled back, "Georgia, and you?"

While waving to get Jacky's attention I said, "I was raised in New York but I live here full-time now." I didn't have much time so I added, "I couldn't help noticing your date. Man-o-man you've got the hottest chick in here."

"Yeah, she is pretty hot." Joey was obviously proud of himself. "I met her yesterday at a grocery store and just started talking to her and I figured what the heck, so I asked her out and here we are."

I encouraged him. "I guess she took one look at you and decided she had to have you."

He laughed. "I guess."

Okay, enough chit-chat, it was time for Joey to leave. I leaned in and spoke in a low voice. "So Dude, how much is she charging you?"

Joey's face was blank. "Huh? Chargin' fer what?"

"You know…" I illustrated by making a circle with my left hand and poking in and out of the circle with the index finger of my right hand. "How much is she charging you for the night?"

Joey went pale. "You mean she's a hooker?"

I shushed him and looked around to make sure no one had heard him. "Of course she's a hooker. Most of the girls in here are hookers. But a girl as hot as yours is in demand and she knows it. Make sure you agree on a price before you take her to a hotel. Got it?"

It took him a few seconds, but Joey finally found his voice. "Wait a minute now. I don't wanna be wit' no damn hooker. I thought she was a nice girl."

I pushed a bit harder. "Joey, what are you talking about? She is nice. In fact, she's the nicest piece of ass in this place. All I'm saying is you don't want to be spending more money than you have to."

Joey started shaking his head. "I can't do this. Shit, what am I gonna do?"

I pretended to be sympathetic. "Oh man, I'm sorry. I thought you knew."

Joey grabbed my hand and shook it. "No man, thanks, you just saved me from makin' a big mistake. I gotta get outta here 'fore she come back. Can you tell her…"

I interrupted. "Don't worry man, I'll take care of it. Us Americans have to stick together, right?"

Joey left a $20 bill on the bar and made a hasty escape. So far, my plan was working perfectly. From here on out it would be easy. I moved over to Joey's stool and waited for his date to come back from the bathroom.

A couple minutes later, she came back to her seat, looked around, and then turned to me and asked, "Excuse me, did you see my friend?"

I turned to her. "You mean Joey? He had to go. He said something about meeting his girlfriend."

The girl was in total shock. "He went to see his girlfriend?"

I continued, "Yes, he asked me to tell you when you got back. He says he's sorry he had to run out so suddenly but he had completely forgotten about his prior engagement."

Her voice was shaky. "I can't believe this."

I looked in her eyes and saw the tears, "Oh, I'm sorry." I reached out and took her hand. "You didn't know about his girlfriend?"

She couldn't talk. She just shook her head slowly as she fought back tears.

"Oh shit, I feel so bad," I said, "but the truth is, you're better off without him. Who knows how many girlfriends he has? These military guys are all the same."

Despite her best efforts, the tears started streaming down her cheeks. "You don't understand, he was my ride home. I have no money. My purse is in his car, and he leaves me stranded here."

I put an angry look on my face. "Fucking bastard! Well honey, don't worry, I'll take care of everything." I had hit the jackpot! She would be spending the night with me. "My name is Xavier. What's yours?"

In a low voice she said, "Nicole."

I turned up the charm. "Well Nicole, you can have anything you want to drink, I'll pay for it. Are you hungry?" Without waiting for an answer, I took her hand and led her towards the restaurant. The bar was so crowded I was sure Nicole was relieved to sit at a private table towards the back of the garden. She had been drinking Presidente beer so I asked the waiter to bring a Presidente for her and a Corona for me. After the waiter left, I reached across the table and took both of her hands in my own. "Nicole, I'm really sorry about that jerk. What can I do to help you put this behind you?"

The tears had stopped, "Thank you Xavier. You've done so much already."

I gave her hands a gentle squeeze, "Don't be silly, all I've done so far is buy you a beer. At least get something to eat."

She looked a little better but something was still bothering her. "I don't know what I'm going to do. I was supposed to spend the night with Joey. I'm staying with friends and everyone is out. They're not expecting me until tomorrow."

Still holding her hands with one of mine, I used the other hand to raise her chin so that I was looking directly into her eyes. "Nicole, everything happens for a reason. You can stay at my house tonight. No strings attached. I'll sleep on the couch, and you can sleep in my bed."

Nicole was shocked. "No way, I can't take your bed."

I interrupted her, "Bottom line is that you're going home with me. We'll discuss sleeping arrangements when we get to my house. But first things first, what are you eating?"

Nicole hesitated. "I don't feel so good. I think I'm gonna throw up."

Looking at her face, I could tell she was serious. I got up from the table, went around to her side, took her hand and led her to the bathroom. The bathroom was being used, but luckily there was no line. Standing in the hallway outside the bathroom, I leaned against the wall and she leaned back into me with my arms wrapped around her as I whispered in her ear. "Hang in there honey, just a little bit longer."

When the door opened, a young woman came out and we went in. I locked the door behind us. Nicole immediately went to her knees and started vomiting into the toilet. Crouching behind her, I spoke comforting words as she emptied her stomach. I put an arm around her lower abdomen to apply gentle pressure and started to rub her back with my free hand. Even then, as my hand rubbed her back, I couldn't help noticing how beautiful her body was. Holding her slender form so closely and looking at her dark chocolate skin, I was tempted to kiss the back of her neck but instead I leaned forward and hugged her. "That's it baby, that's it, get it all out."

When she was done, I helped her to her feet and led her to the sink. She rinsed out her mouth and washed her face, then took the paper towel I was holding for her. I was standing behind her as she looked at my reflection in the mirror above the sink. "Thank you." Her voice was so soft, it was as though she had mouthed the words.

"Are you okay?" I asked with genuine concern.

As she turned to face me, she nodded her head. "Yes, I'm a little embarrassed but I'll live. We went to the beach. I've been drinking all day. I guess I had a little too much."

I held her by the shoulders, looked into her eyes and started in a clear voice, "Well, I'll take care of you. Maybe I can get them to make you some soup or something to settle your stomach." The last few words were barely audible as I leaned forward and kissed her. It was a gentle kiss placed delicately on her lips.

She started to kiss back then pulled away and turned her face to the side. "I'm so embarrassed. You must think I'm so disgusting."

I laughed a bit, "Trust me, I've kissed much worse." Then I got serious as I took her chin again and looked into her eyes, "Actually I enjoyed it very much."

She leaned forward, put her head on my chest and hugged me. "Thank you. I don't know what I'd be doing now if you hadn't come along."

Of course, I knew if I hadn't come along she'd be having a great time with Joey, but that was my secret. "Okay," I said, "let's get you something to eat."

We walked out holding hands as I led her back to our table. Unfortunately, the only way there was, was through the bar, so everyone saw us go to and from the bathroom, but I didn't care. I was genuinely attracted to this girl and I wasn't gonna let anyone stop me from getting to know her better. When the waiter came, I explained the situation and he said he knew just the thing for her and walked away.

Nicole looked at me with a puzzled expression. "What is he bringing me?"

I smiled, "Don't worry, whatever it is, it'll be exactly what you need."

We passed the time with me asking her general questions about what she did and who she knew. It turned out she was seventeen years old and had only been to the Flamenco a few times to see Freddy play on Thursday nights. She didn't get out much and had no boyfriend. When she ran into Joey at a grocery store near her house, they got into a conversation when he asked her to translate the labels on the items he was trying to buy. He had seemed so nice that when he offered to drive her home, she accepted and when he asked if she wanted to go to the beach with him the next day, she had been flattered. Of course, I knew the rest of the story.

Fifteen minutes later, the waiter came back with a bowl of bread soup and a glass of tomato juice. Nicole thanked the waiter and I encouraged her to eat as much as she could. While she ate, I drank and we talked. Several hours later, we were still talking and I even had her laughing. Joey was just a distant memory. But it was time to go home. Since it was after two in the morning, calling a driver from work was out of the question. Nelson was away for the weekend and my stepfather would be fast asleep. We walked to the bar and I tried several times to get through to Nick's Taxi Service without success. When I asked Bryan about it, he told me that Nick's was closed for a week. Apparently, a driver had been shot. That was not what I wanted to hear.

I turned to Nicole. "Well babe, I have good news and bad news."

Nicole looked worried. "Give me the good news first."

I smiled, "The good news is you're still more than welcome to sleep over."

"And the bad news?" she asked.

I frowned, "The bad news is it looks like we have to walk."

Nicole perked up. "That's it?"

"Well, I live kind of far," I said.

"How far?" she asked.

"Down to Delmas 75 and about three miles in." I answered.

Nicole considered for a moment, then said, "Well actually, that's not too bad, and a lot closer than my house."

"Well, that settles it," I said, "let's go."

We started walking through downtown Pétion-Ville and around the market where all the major roads converged. From there, we followed Delmas road down to Delmas 75. The entire time we joked and laughed, so the time passed quickly. When we started down Delmas 75, Nicole's mood changed. The road was mostly dark and the light poles were few and far between. I actually knew it was safer walking in the dark and would have preferred to stay in the shadows but I didn't want to say anything to scare Nicole more than she already was. I held her hand and kept up a conversation. Eventually, we got to the tiny cemetery near my house. When Nicole spotted the burial vaults, she grabbed my arm and shrieked.

"What's wrong?" I asked.

She was trembling. "A cemetery!"

I didn't quite understand. "Yes, my house is around the corner and at the top of the hill."

She looked at me in disbelief. "You actually live near a cemetery? Aren't you scared?"

Now it was my turn to have a look of disbelief. "Why should I be scared? They're dead." To illustrate my point I started pulling her towards the cemetery.

Nicole yanked herself free, ran to the other side of the street and begged me. "Xavier please! Get me away from this place."

The entire scene seemed so ridiculous to me that I felt an object lesson was in order. "Look, I'll show you how harmless it is." And with that I jumped up onto the closest vault and started to dance. I jumped from one vault to another singing, dancing and making a total fool of myself until I noticed that Nicole was crying. Only then did I realize what I was doing and jumped back down and walked across the street to her. "Nicole, I'm sorry. Don't be scared. I was just being stupid."

Nicole was shaking in terror. "Please Xavier; just get me away from here."

We walked quickly the rest of the way to my house. Quietly, I opened the gate and we made our way inside to my room. Once inside, Nicole threw her arms around me and held me tight. Her heart was beating fast. I felt like such an idiot and I tried to apologize but Nicole stopped me with a kiss. Soon we were tearing our clothes off until we were both naked. I scooped her up in my arms, laid her on the bed and started kissing her neck as I fondled her breasts. Normally, I would have teased her and played with her until she begged me to fuck her, but my desire was too strong. I inserted two fingers inside her and confirmed that she was wet and ready. Hurriedly, I got a condom from the nightstand and put it on.

When I slipped inside her she whispered in my ear, "Oh yes, finally. I've been waiting for this all night."

I had been waiting too and wasted no time getting us both to climax. We were both too tired to do anything fancy, but we nonetheless enjoyed the feeling and fell fast asleep in each other's arms.

It was around noon when I opened my eyes. I was pretty badly hung over and disoriented. At first, I thought it was Mickey with her arms around me and her head on my chest. Then I remembered it was Nicole. I put a hand on her ass. For such a tiny girl she had a very impressive ass. I gave her whole body a squeeze and she hugged me back. Despite my aching head, it felt great to hold her in my arms. As gently as I could, I slid out from under her and went to the bathroom. After relieving myself, I found Mary and told her to prepare breakfast for me and a guest. Pop was sitting in the upper courtyard reading a newspaper and sipping his rum on ice. I kissed him on the forehead and sat in a chair next to him. "Morning Pop."

"Morning to you too," he said. "How was your night?"

I looked at him and smiled, "I don't remember much so it must have been pretty good."

Pop laughed. "Does that mean someone will be joining you for breakfast?"

I liked Nicole and I wanted to see her again so the last thing I wanted was for Pop to embarrass her. "Pop, please, I'm asking you nicely, can you please not say anything to make her feel bad? She's a nice girl."

"What the hell are you talking about?" Pop's face changed to a mix of annoyance and disgust. "I'm sure she's a very nice girl," he said sarcastically, "Does she usually sleep out or is that just with you? Look son, fuck whoever you want, as much as you want, but you can't bring these tramps into this house and expect me to treat them with respect."

It was hopeless. "You're right Pop. I'm sorry." And with that I got up and went inside. Mary had set two places at the table in the kitchen. I asked her to bring the food to my room instead and went downstairs. Nicole was sitting in bed holding her head. After kissing her, I gave her a towel and showed her the bathroom. When she got back from her shower, breakfast was waiting for her. While she ate, I took my turn in the shower. When I got back, Nicole was dressed and sitting on the edge of the bed. I had no intention of letting her go just yet. "And where do you think you're going?" I asked.

"It's time for me to go home," she said.

"I'm sorry," I joked, "last night was just foreplay. I can't let you go until I've made proper love to you. I have a reputation, you know."

"Oh, I know," she said.

Something in the tone of her voice caught my attention. "What do you mean you know?"

Nicole looked at me, "I've been wanting to meet you for a while. I've heard so much about you. But I didn't want to get too close." She paused to gauge my reaction.

I was confused. "What do you mean?"

"You dated my best friend," she said, "she's the one who first told me about you."

I fucked a lot of women, but dating was not something I did very often. "What's your friend's name?"

Nicole hesitated. "Her name is Patricia."

I almost choked. "You're friends with Pattie?"

Seeing my reaction caused Nicole to freeze, but when she saw the questioning look she continued. "Pattie is my best friend in the world. She's like a sister to me. If she knew I slept with you she would die."

Suddenly I was very disappointed. "So Pattie told you about me?"

Nicole answered carefully. "Yes, but I wanted to see you for myself. I've seen you at the Flamenco a few times, but I kept my distance. I was so scared when I saw you sitting at the bar in Joey's seat."

"Why would you be scared?" I wondered out loud.

"They say you've slept with every girl in there and I didn't want to be just another notch in your belt."

Pop was right. Nicole was just another tramp, and furthermore, she most definitely was just another notch in my belt. But even as I tried to convince myself of this, I could feel that there was something different about her. "You're not anything like Pattie; how did you two end up being friends?"

"Long, boring story," Nicole replied. "But tell me, why did you break up with her?"

I looked at Nicole. "I have one very simple rule and she broke it. Do you know what that rule is?"

Nicole shook her head.

"Absolutely no talking to my ex-wife. Don't you think that's simple?"

Nicole nodded.

"But not only does your best friend talk to my ex-wife, she's fucking my ex-wife. But of course, you know that."

Nicole shook her head, "I don't see Pattie as often as I used to. I know she's living with a woman named Alice, but I didn't know she was your wife."

"Ex-wife, damn it! Get it right!"

"I'm sorry." Nicole offered.

I had wanted to make love to her again before taking her home; only this time go slow and give her a proper fix, but my mood was ruined. I took off my robe, threw it on the bed, and turned towards the closet to find some clothes. As I stood there naked, looking through my closet, with my back to Nicole, I suddenly felt her hands on my back.

"I'm sorry," she said, "don't be upset." When I turned to face her, she kissed me and an uncontrollable wave of desire swept over me. I undressed her and we made love.

Chapter 7
"Butterflies"

One afternoon, as I waited in the motor pool for my ride home, Jean, the dispatcher, struck up a conversation. At first, I thought it was small talk, but I soon realized that he was trying to make a point.

"Xavier," he started, "I've been watching you for a long time and I can see that you're not happy."

"Really?" I replied, "and how do you see that?"

"Well, it's no secret that your wife was trouble." Jean was right. Alice had more than once caused a scene at work. In the most recent incident, she had commandeered the vehicle I was to take on a trip to one of our field offices. I listened as Jean continued. "A man like you needs a good woman by his side. Are you seeing anyone?"

"No," I replied.

"Then how can you be happy?" he asked. "Every man needs a good woman."

"Are you kidding?" I said, "There's no such thing as a good woman. Besides, I'm perfectly happy being single."

Jean leaned forward and in a quiet voice said, "Xavier, I know this really nice girl and I think the two of you might hit it off really well."

I was suspicious but intrigued. "What does she look like?"

"Xavier," Jean said with a smile, "do you really think I would waste your time?"

"I suppose not," I answered, "but if she's so hot, why aren't you with her?"

"Can't touch her," he said as he shook his head. "She's my girl-friend's little cousin. But she's a nice girl and we talk. Just the other day she was saying how hard it is to find a nice guy, and I thought of you."

"Really?" I said, with a raised eyebrow. "That's very nice of you Jean." And with a smile I added, "So when do I meet this lucky girl?"

Jean thought about it and then said, "I can have her stop by the office if you want, then the two of you can take it from there."

"Sounds good," I said. "Have her stop by Thursday afternoon."

Two days later, I arrived at work feeling very tired and walked into my office with a yawn. The large monthly calendar on the wall behind my desk was several months old. My desk was crowded with obsolete project proposals, technical manuals, trade journals, computer magazines, and a few parts, some broken and some new. I made room for my notebook computer, opened it, leaned back in my chair and considered the wording of an important memo I needed to send out to all of our field offices as I waited for it to boot.

A young woman in a tidy uniform with a white head scarf and apron opened the sliding glass door and entered my office. "Good morning Mr. Xavier." She placed my over-sized ceramic mug on the small warmer and switched it on. Next to the mug she put a small package of crackers, and a small package of cookies.

I smiled. "Good morning Lucy, how are you?"

She smiled back and said, "Doing good Mr. Xavier. It's always good when the weekend is this close."

"My goodness, is it Thursday already?" I asked.

"Yes it is," she replied. "Isn't it amazing how time flies?"

"Yes," I said, looking into her eyes, "amazing indeed." Lucy was already working for The Agency when I started. She was young, pretty and caught my eye immediately. Since then, she had given birth to several children and gained a lot of weight, but I still found her pretty, especially when she smiled at me.

Lucy was smiling quite radiantly. "Can I get you anything else, Mr. Xavier?"

I looked at the items she had placed on my desk, "I have my coffee, my snacks..." then I looked at her, "...and I'm starting the day with your beautiful smile. What else could I possibly want?" I looked around my office then looked back into her eyes with a sly grin. "Oh, I know. Can you stop calling me Mr. Xavier? Just Xavier is fine, unless of course you feel more comfortable calling me honey or darling."

Lucy giggled. "Yes, Mr. Just Xavier darling. I'll get to work on that right away," she said, as she pulled a slip of paper from her pocket and placed it on my desk. "I like that, it has a nice ring to it."

I reached for my wallet as I laughed. "Okay, I get the point, but you can't blame me for trying." I didn't even need to look at the note. My snacks amounted to $1.50 a day and I still owed her for the previous week. I pulled $25 from my wallet and handed it to her. "Lucy... darling, I seem to have a bit of an appetite this morning. When you are done with your rounds, can you bring me a lightly toasted, buttered bagel?"

Lucy put the money in her pocket. She was avoiding my eyes and suppressing a giggle. "Yes, Mr. Xavier." She turned quickly and left my office.

I hadn't even taken a sip of my coffee yet and I was feeling energized. Amazing how a pretty smile and a little flirting could get a man's day started just right.

That afternoon I got a call from Nadine, the receptionist. "Xavier, you have someone here to see you."

I could tell from her voice that she was smiling. Nadine was about my age and had been with The Agency for what seemed like forever. I felt a little sorry for her because she was so good at her job that I was sure she'd be our receptionist for life. When it came to women, I didn't discriminate, I loved them all, but Nadine was very much the type of woman I preferred: cute face, even-toned skin a shade darker than mine, slim waist, nice ass, a generous bosom, jet black hair down past her shoulders and the cutest little feet. We flirted constantly, but it was all in fun. In truth, she was a good friend and something of a confidante. Like many people, she assumed a good woman in my life was what I needed. Hey, that was fine with me. I was perfectly willing to sample any woman that came my way, but if people were volunteering to recruit for me, I certainly wasn't going to discourage them.

I put Nadine on speakerphone and leaned back in my chair. "What does she look like?"

"Very nice," Nadine said, "cute girl in her early twenties, professionally dressed, very well-spoken," and after a pause, "and it looks like she just got her nails done. Xavier, you didn't tell me you were interviewing. Are you keeping secrets from me?"

"Nadine, you know very well there are no openings in my department," I said.

Nadine cleared her throat and in a confidential tone said, "Now Xavier, we both know that's not the kind of interview I was talking about." Then regaining her professional voice, she added, "Anyway, should I send the young lady to your office?"

I looked around at the mess. "Oh no," I said quickly, "tell her I'll be right there."

"Very well then," she said before hanging up.

When I got to the lobby, I saw a very attractive girl sitting upright on the couch. Her feet were planted firmly on the floor, her knees were together and both hands were on her knees. She wore a Navy blue skirt and a white blouse. Her hair was done up in a bun. If she were here for a job, she would definitely score extra points for her appearance and demeanor. She was a small girl with caramel colored skin. The shape of her nose and chin made her look a bit like Liza Minnelli but her hair was obviously longer. Not bad for a first impression. I walked towards her with a smile and extended my hand. "You must be Elizabeth." As she stood up to take my hand, I pulled her towards me and kissed her on both cheeks.

"And you must be Xavier," she said. "Jean has told me so much about you."

Still holding her hand, I put on a look of mock indignation. "Don't believe a word he said, I'm not nearly as bad as all that." With a grin, I added, "And I almost never bite."

She laughed, "Actually, Jean said some very nice things about you."

"Really?" I said sounding surprised. "Like what?"

"Well," she started, "he actually said quite a lot, so I decided that I just had to meet you and see for myself."

"And I'm glad you did," I said. "Now that I see you, I don't mind the $50 he charged me to say all those nice things." At that, we both laughed. "So Elizabeth, let me take you for a tour." I turned to Nadine as I spoke, "You've already met the most important person here. Nadine runs this place." I winked at Nadine and she smiled back at us.

Elizabeth smiled at Nadine, picked up her purse and said, "Oh, I'd love to, but I can't stay, my ride is waiting for me."

"Your ride?" I asked.

Elizabeth opened her purse and started looking through it, "Yes, he's waiting in the parking lot, but I wanted to give you this." She pulled a small envelope from her purse and handed it to me. My full name was written out in beautiful, hand-written calligraphy. It was obviously an invitation. "I hope you can come, it's this Sunday. It's a First Communion banquet for one of my cousins."

"I'd be happy to come." I said.

Elizabeth produced a pen from her purse, "Here, let me write my phone number on the back."

I handed her the envelope and as she wrote her number, I pulled out my wallet, took out a business card and wrote my home number on it. "So I don't see you 'til Sunday?" I asked, purposely sounding disappointed.

"We can see each other before then," she said. "Just call me." She gave me back the envelope.

I handed her my business card. "That's my home number on the back. Why don't we have lunch tomorrow? Just tell me where to pick you up."

She thought about it a moment before replying. "What time do you get off work?"

"Well," I replied, "the office closes at three-thirty, but I never leave before five. What do you have in mind?"

"I'd love to have lunch with you," she said, "but I have several job interviews in the afternoon and they're all downtown. But I can be here around five and you can take me home, that way you'll know where to pick me up on Sunday."

I offered her my arm. "That works. Let me walk you to the parking lot."

A few minutes later, I walked back into the building with a huge grin on my face. Nadine couldn't help laughing.

"So what do you think?" I asked.

"She's okay," Nadine said.

"Don't worry darling, you know you're still number one." And with that, I leaned over her desk and gave her a quick peck on the cheek.

Nadine was taken totally off guard. "Xavier, are you crazy?"

I just laughed and went back to my office.

I was feeling very upbeat. Usually, I couldn't wait until three-thirty because it meant the office would clear out and I could work until six or seven without my phone ringing. But that day I couldn't wait until three-thirty because I just wanted to go out and have fun. There was a weird feeling deep down inside. A strange feeling like butterflies in my stomach. It felt vaguely familiar. It felt good.

That night at the Flamenco, I saw Nicole. She was looking good as always, but my mind was on Elizabeth. Nicole sat next to me at the bar and I bought her a drink. We talked for a bit and even made plans to go to the beach together. "Maybe next weekend," I had said. A day at the beach would do me good. Besides, there was something unsettling about my attraction to Elizabeth. There I was, sitting with Nicole, and I was thinking of Elizabeth. To clear my mind I leaned forward and kissed Nicole on the lips. The kiss was brief and Nicole didn't even have a chance to react.

"What was that for?" she asked.

"Just for being you," I said. I knew Nicole was in love with me and deep down I knew my attraction to her was more than just physical, but I wouldn't let her get too close. I had made a big mistake with Pattie and unfortunately, Nicole was paying for it. I was tempted to take her home with me. I knew all I had to do was ask and she would say yes. But it was a week night and I had to work the next day. I leaned forward and kissed her again. This time she kissed me back. The kiss was short but kissing her there in plain sight of everyone was stupid. I stood up and squeezed her hand discreetly. "I have to go. I'll see you this weekend." And I started to walk away.

The desire in Nicole's eyes had been pretty obvious. "Xavier."

I turned to faced her. "Yes Nicole?"

The look faded slowly and was replaced with one of resignation and a weak smile. "Never mind, I'll see you this weekend."

I turned, left the restaurant and went home.

The following day, Elizabeth arrived at about 4:45. I quickly packed my notebook computer and met her in the lobby. I radioed the dispatcher and a couple minutes later one of the mechanics drove up to the front office in a white Jeep Wrangler, got out and handed me the keys. I opened the passenger door for Elizabeth and helped her in. "How were your interviews?" I asked, once I was in the driver's seat.

"Pretty good," she said. "I have a really good feeling about one of them."

"Are you hungry?" I asked. "We can have dinner before going to your house."

Elizabeth smiled at me, "I have a better idea, why don't we go to my house? Then I can change clothes and we can spend more time together."

"Perfect," I said with a smile. Elizabeth was staying with her cousin, Jean's girlfriend, in a small house thirty minutes up the mountain. It was a nice drive. As I took in the familiar scenery, I realized that it had been a couple of months since I'd gone off-road dirt-biking. Of course my broken neck had a lot to do with it, but I should be able to ride my motorcycle if I was careful and didn't push myself too hard. With that in mind, I made a mental note to get my motorcycle from the motor pool the next day

While Liz got dressed, Jean's girlfriend kept me company. I was doing most of the talking as I told her about the development projects we had in different parts of the country. When Liz came out, my eyes nearly popped out of their sockets. She was wearing a short-sleeve, form-fitting, capri jumpsuit made of stretch denim, with a zipper going down the front. The zipper was low enough to show plenty of cleavage. Her hair was loose and flowed past her shoulders onto her back and chest. To keep it casual and highlight her small size, Liz chose to wear white leather thong sandals with no heel. It was the first time I had seen her toes and they were absolutely beautiful. The semi-clear polish on her toenails had the iridescence of pearl and caught the light in the most fascinating way as she walked past us and into the kitchen. As she did, my eyes locked onto her ass and I imagined all the ways I wanted to have her. From the absence of a panty line, I knew the thongs on Liz' feet were not the only ones she was wearing. I was in total lust.

That evening I took Liz to Harry's, a casual place far from my usual hang-outs. We had burgers, fries and good conversation as we got to know each other. Elizabeth was reserved and of a quiet, easy-going temperament with a lot of class. Even so, she seized every opportunity to show me her playful and funny side. The chemistry was there and we both knew it. I didn't want the night to end, but I couldn't wait to kiss her. After dinner, we went out for ice cream. Wanting to maintain my image as the perfect gentleman, I kept my eye on the time. It was thirty minutes back up the mountain and I wanted to make sure I had her home by midnight. Liz was surprised when I announced at eleven-fifteen that it was time to go home, but I got a smile out of her when I explained I didn't want her cousin to get a bad impression of me.

We got to her house with five minutes to spare. Liz went in to let her cousin know she was home and came back out to the car. When she got in the passenger seat, I took her hand and held it as I told her what a wonderful time I had. Then we looked in each other's eyes for a brief moment. I could tell she wanted me to kiss her, but I didn't want to seem too eager. I put her hand near my face, turned it palm up, kissed her palm and closed her fingers around my kiss. I smiled at her and told her I had to go. I promised to call her the next day and I walked her to the door. Once there, she leaned with her back against the door and just looked at me. I had to kiss her. Slowly, I closed the distance between us and held both her hands at her sides with our fingers intertwined. I closed my eyes and moved in. My lips brushed hers very softly until I felt her lips curl up into a smile, then I kissed her. It felt like it could have lasted forever, but I wanted to leave her wanting more so I took a step back, smiled, promised to call her, released her hands and turned to walk away.

It had been a perfect date, but I needed an adrenaline rush so I timed myself racing down the narrow mountain road and back to the Flamenco. Less than seventeen minutes later, I was in front of the restaurant. I had a few drinks but somehow, after an evening with Liz, the Flamenco seemed like a step down, so I went home.

The next day, Saturday, I went to the motor pool and got my motorcycle. That was my favorite form of transportation. Since I was the only assigned rider, my blue and black Suzuki was exactly where I had left it more than a month earlier. If I ever needed a jeep, all I had to do was ask for one, which is what I usually requested for the weekends. Because of my neck, I hadn't ridden in a month. I barely even drove. But being chauffeured around was getting lame and that day, I definitely wanted to feel the rush of air.

I rode for several hours far up into the mountains that overlooked the bay of Port-au-Prince and away from any roads. I rode until even the trails became nothing more than goat paths. I rode until there were no homes and no sign of human presence. The further up I went, the cooler it got. Lord, it felt good to breathe crisp, clean, mountain air!

When I was far enough up the mountain that an encounter with another human was almost impossible, I got off the bike and sat on a boulder. I lit a cigarette and looked off into the distance. Through the haze I could see the island of La Gonave; just a formless blotch of grayish brown, competing with the setting sun for my attention. It was no contest. La Gonave didn't stand a chance. But as the sun started to set, it made a token gesture to the island by highlighting its edges with a temporary crown of fiery red. It was time to ride home.

I prepared myself for the adrenaline rush that was to come. I was far from any road and soon it would be dark. I had to ride hard and fast through fields, hills, valleys, and ravines while there was still light. I decided on the most dangerous route. Rather than go back the way I had come, I would take the long way, forward over this mountain and down the other side to the very bottom and take the dry riverbed back to town. It was a crazy thing to do, all the more so because I had no protective gear other than my helmet. It didn't even occur to me that I had so recently broken my neck and I was supposed to be taking it easy.

The race was on as I gunned the throttle and tore up the grassy mountainside looking for any shortcut to the top. Every second was precious. I had to fly, and fly is what I did. At almost no time were both wheels on the ground together and quite often I would be soaring through the air, using any available surface as a ramp. The feeling was wonderful; I was getting high off the adrenaline flowing freely though my body as I maneuvered my bike across the landscape. When I flew over the top and started my descent down the other side, my momentum, gravity, and the terrain all conspired to force me into a straight line down the steep mountainside, but that would have meant certain death. I fought the mountain, pulling first to the right, then to the left, zigzagging my way down the slope. As I rode, only one mistake away from serious injury or worse, I couldn't help thinking: If I were to fall and die what a glorious end it would be! We all had to die sooner or later, but to die on my terms, that would be something indeed. I clenched my teeth and pushed the death wish out of my mind. Some day, perhaps some day soon, but not that day! I had no intentions of surrendering my life to this mountain. I rode for all I was worth, racing not only against the mountain, but also against the setting sun.

When I made it to the riverbed, I was faced with a different challenge. The terrain was mostly gravel and loose rocks so I could go fast, but in many ways it was more dangerous because as I followed the serpentine bends of the dry river, there were surprises around every corner. The sun, then fully set, gave way to a new enemy as dusk set in. Seeing the giant boulders was easy enough, but the large rocks were much harder to see, and spotting the occasional holes in the river bottom became impossible. It would only get worse as darkness, my most powerful enemy, was preparing to relieve the dusk in this fight to claim my life. I had to ride harder and faster, but the faster I rode, the more likely I was to smash my bike and myself against the rocks.

Finally, as light started to fail, I saw the landmark I had been looking for, a steep footpath leading up and out of the river. I steered hard to the left and gunned the throttle to pick up speed and momentum for the abrupt climb up and out. As I cleared the end of the path, I gave the throttle an extra kick and caught some air before landing on a street in a residential neighborhood on the edge of town. I had made it! The exhilarating rush was beyond description. I was out of danger but I couldn't relax yet. Several blocks later, I was on a main road weaving through heavy traffic, accompanied by all the noises of the metropolis.

Sometime later, I was home. My first priority was to grab a cold beer from the fridge. I was filthy and needed a shower, but I had a bigger problem. Once the adrenaline started to wear off, I realized that I was in terrible pain and I couldn't turn my neck. Riding so hard had definitely been a bad idea. After my shower, I put my neck brace on, got high and went to sleep.

When I woke up the next day, I realized that I hadn't called Liz. My neck was still stiff, but there was no way I was going to let her down. In fact, I needed to hear her voice, so I called. "Good evening, could I speak to Elizabeth?"

"Xavier? Hi!" Liz sounded excited, "I thought you were going to call yesterday."

"I'm sorry," I said, "I went riding and I hurt my neck. I wanted to call you, but I was in so much pain that I took a sedative and slept through the night."

The concern in Liz' voice was unmistakable. "Oh! Are you okay?"

I smiled as I spoke. "I'm a little stiff but I'll be fine. What time should I pick you up?"

Reassured that I was okay, she replied. "Well, you can pick me up at six."

"Okay, see you then," I said.

When I picked her up, Liz looked radiant. She was in a little black cocktail dress with sexy black sandals. The two straps across the feet were black velvet and the one around her ankles was studded with faux diamonds. Add the four-inch stiletto heels and the entire outfit whispered seductively to my perverted imagination.

The banquet wasn't far from my house. I wasn't normally a fan of such events, but Liz and I danced all night and we had a great time. When it was over, we went to Boutillier, a lookout point just above the town of Pétion-Ville. It was a common place to come at night due to the breathtaking view of the metropolis. From up there it looked like a carpet of lights rolling down the mountain and spilling into the ocean. There were a few other cars, but we found a spot that was reasonably private despite the light of the full moon. When I parked the car, I stepped out, went around to the passenger side and opened the door. Liz turned to exit the jeep but I blocked her. She looked up into my eyes as I leaned forward. I stopped only a few inches from her face and paused. Liz was ready for a kiss but I smiled slightly, started to move back, and said, "I should take you home."

Liz looked confused, "We don't have to go yet." When she realized I was still moving slowly backwards, she reached out with one swift movement and grabbed my tie. She didn't pull but she kept me from moving further back.

I put my hands lightly on her knees. "But it's getting late."

Liz had a pleading yet tender look in her eye as she replied. "It's not that late."

Slowly and softly, I started to rake my fingernails up her delicate thighs. When I got to the fabric of her dress, I kept raking and in the process pushed the dress further and further up. "But this is only our second date; I wouldn't want you to get the wrong idea."

I could see her breathing quicken and she pulled a bit on my tie. "I don't think you need to worry about that, Xavier."

I let her pull me in a few inches, then resisted. At this point I had the dress up as high as it would go. I moved my fingers to her inner thighs and slowly started raking back down the inside using my fingertips this time. "I don't know Elizabeth, I mean, we hardly know each other."

She pulled a bit more on my tie and started to lean forward to steal a kiss. "So this is our chance to get to know each other."

I looked down at her legs and as I started my fingers back up her inner thighs, I followed with my eyes until I was staring at her black lace panties. "Yes, there are definitely some things I want to know more about."

She pulled a bit harder on the tie. "Like what?"

I moved my right hand quickly to her panties and pressed several fingers against the moist material as I made eye contact with her again. "Like what turns you on…"

Her mouth opened in a silent "Oh" as she let go of the tie, leaned back and used both hands to brace herself against the seat.

I moved forward and grabbed her tiny torso with both hands, in such a way that my thumbs came to rest on her nipples. "…what makes you feel good…"

Her eyes started to close. "Oh my!"

I lifted her up slightly as I massaged her nipples. "…how you want to be touched."

Realizing I was supporting her, Liz used both hands to pull her dress out from under her and up around her waist. "Touch me any way you want, Xavier."

Now that her dress was partially out of the way, I moved in close, wrapped my arms around her and kissed her neck, then her ear before whispering, "But I want to see more."

Liz put her hands on my chest and pushed me gently back. "You want to see my body?"

I started caressing her inner thighs with my fingers. "Yes."

She slowly and deliberately pushed the left strap off her shoulder. "You want to see me naked?"

I looked deep into her eyes. "Yes."

She pushed the right strap off her shoulder and smiled at me. "So what are you waiting for?"

I moved in slowly and went for her neck. As I started kissing up to her ear, then down her cheek and along the line of her chin, my fingers teased her nipples through the thin material of her dress. Liz wasn't wearing a bra; she didn't need one. Her small breasts were firm and fit perfectly in the palms of my hands. When I heard her start to moan, I pulled down the top of her dress so that the whole dress was gathered around her waist. Since she was then completely exposed, I found her hands and stepped back. Still holding her hands, I looked at her in the moonlight. I smiled, first admiring the delicate features of her face, and then looked down at her breasts. Her tiny nipples pointed just slightly upwards. After a moment, I released one of her hands, touched the space between her breasts with one finger and traced a zigzag downward as my eyes followed my finger down to her navel. I leaned back a bit to look at her thighs. Struck by the sight of her body, I said in a soft voice, "Damn baby, you're so beautiful."

When I looked up, she was smiling. "No one has ever looked at me like that before."

I started moving slowly towards her again. "You have the most amazing body. I want to look at it like that every day. Let's make that happen."

At that point, Liz took my hand, brought it to her face and kissed it, "I'm yours for as long as you'll have me."

I moved in quickly and planted a kiss on her lips. She responded by wrapping her arms around me as we searched for each other's tongues. While still locked in a passionate kiss, I broke free of her arms and pulled off my jacket with all the urgency that the situation called for and tossed it onto the driver's seat. Next, I loosened my tie. When Liz realized what I was doing, she started unbuttoning my shirt. Once she had loosened the last button, we separated long

LOVERS ANONYMOUS

enough for our eyes to meet. We seemed to be thinking the same thought as we wondered how far this would go. Liz made the next move by leaning forward and locking her mouth onto my left nipple while rolling my right one between her thumb and forefinger. Caught off guard, I let out a moan. Liz was then in control of the situation, and I relished the feeling, even as my knees started to quiver. All I could say was, "Holy shit!"

Realizing she had the upper hand, Liz continued sucking on my nipple but used her other hand to search my body. She went straight for my zipper, reached into my pants, and grabbed my shaft through my briefs. Hearing me moan a bit louder emboldened her. Liz released her suction grip on my nipple and pushed me back, then jumped out of the jeep, turned us around and pushed me so my back was against the side of the vehicle. With a swift movement, she unbuckled my belt and my pants fell down to my ankles. Once my slacks were out of the way, she pressed her body against me with surprising force considering her small frame. We locked lips again. I wrapped my arms around her, picked her up and turned us so that her back was against the jeep. Liz responded by wrapping her legs around me. Using the side of the jeep as a backboard, I ground my pelvis against hers. I wanted to drop my briefs and impale her on the spot. There was absolutely no doubt in my mind that she wanted to fuck as bad as I did, but it didn't feel right. I had done so much fucking and I wanted this to be different. Liz was special, not like all those other women, and I wanted her to feel special. I slowed my grind and tried to break the kiss.

In frustration, Liz made a plaintive sound as she tried to reconnect with my mouth. "Baby, please don't stop." But as she looked at my face, she could see the seriousness, and unlocked her legs from my waist. "Honey, what's wrong?"

I lowered her gently to the ground. "Baby, I want this too, I want it so bad I'm gonna bust, but not here, not like this. You deserve better than this. When we do it the first time, I want it to be special.

I want to make it special for you every time we do it, because you are special."

She looked up at me. "You're serious."

It almost sounded like a question and I suddenly thought maybe I was sending the wrong signals. "Baby, I care so much about you. When we do it, I want it to be some place nice. I want to make it something you remember forever."

Liz put a hand to her mouth and the moonlight reflected off the gathering pools perched on the edges of her lower eyelids. "Oh my god." She buried her face in my chest, wrapped her arms around me and repeated again very softly, "Oh my god."

For a moment, I wasn't sure what was going on. "Honey, I'm sorry, I didn't mean to upset you…" Beyond that I was at a total loss for words.

With her face still pressed against my chest, Liz let out a little laugh and said, "Xavier Pierre, Jr., you are the most adorable man in the world." She leaned back to look at me as she added, "And I am the luckiest woman in the world."

I let out a sigh of relief. "I thought you were upset."

With her arms still wrapped around me she kissed my chest. "Xavier, you can have me anyway you want, anytime you want and it will be special."

I knew exactly how I wanted to do it. "Spend the weekend with me."

Liz smiled, "Baby, the weekend is over, you're going to work tomorrow."

I smiled back, "I mean next weekend. Spend the whole weekend with me at the Villa Creole. Please say yes."

Liz looked totally surprised. "Wow, that's big. The whole week-end? At the Villa Creole? Are you sure Xavier?"

I repeated again, "Please say yes."

Liz smiled from ear to ear. "Of course I'll spend the weekend with you."

It then occurred to me that we must have been quite a sight under the moonlight: her dress around her waist and my pants around my ankles. "Baby, let's get back in the car."

We fixed our clothes and got back in the jeep. Once inside I looked at Liz, "You do understand, right?"

She just nodded her head with a dreamy look in her eyes.

I started the car and took her home. Of course, we made out some more in front of her house. Eventually, I got back home but I was in some serious discomfort. I needed release bad. I was starting to think that not popping Liz might have been a very stupid mistake, but the romantic side of me took over and decided this would only make the relationship stronger. Still, I had a serious problem on my hands. Fucking another woman was out of the question. Then I came up with an idea. I got high, and masturbated, which is something I seldom did. As I relived the events from Boutillier, I had one massive drug-induced orgasm after another and the best night's sleep in a very long time.

Chapter 8
"The Villa Creole"

That week we talked on the phone everyday and finally Friday came. At four o'clock, Liz arrived at the office with a small suitcase and I had a driver take us to the hotel.

The Villa Creole was a wonderful place. Although near the heart of Pétion-Ville, everything was designed to give a feeling of secluded luxury. A private road led off the main street and past the El Rancho Hotel, another landmark of the city. One Sunday a month, I would spend the day at the Villa. Almost always I came alone and stayed all day drinking, resting, and sometimes reading by the pool until well after sunset. I would have lunch by the pool and an elegant dinner in the dining room. This was the one place where even though the staff all knew me by name, I made no effort to know theirs. I was always polite but I went there to get away from everyone, not to socialize. The Villa was my secret hideout. The only exception was Sam, the bartender. Being on a first-name basis with the man who poured my drinks was an absolute necessity for someone who depended on booze as much as I did.

The driver parked under the canopy and I helped Liz out of the Jeep. The entrance to the hotel was a showcase of elegant Mediterranean style with distinctly Haïtian accents. All the wrought iron gates and security bars throughout the hotel were decorated with intricate patterns in the shapes of hearts, crosses, and stars, the traditional symbols of Haïtian folklore. Contrasting nicely with the iron work around the lobby were paintings by Haïtian masters. The lobby may have been the showcase, but the entire hotel was an art gallery. While Liz looked at the paintings, I walked up to the front desk and the manager on duty, a very professional looking young woman, greeted me with a smile. "Well, Mr. Pierre, I see you'll be spending the entire weekend with us. Please let me know if there is anything I can do for you."

As I signed in, I said, "I'm sure everything will be perfect as always, but if I need anything I won't hesitate." I was about to walk away when I had a thought. I turned back and flashed a quick look at her name badge. "Actually, there is something: flowers. Can you have the room filled with flowers? And a bottle of champagne, of course."

"Mr. Pierre, flowers on such short notice..." The manager looked in Liz' direction and then smiled at me. "Let me see what I can do."

I was relieved and very grateful. "Thank you, Maude. I really appreciate this. Use your discretion and put it all on my account."

Maude couldn't hide her surprise. In the two years she had worked at the Villa it was the first time I had ever referred to her by name. "Of course, Mr. Pierre. Always a pleasure to serve one of our best clients."

"How much time do you need?" I asked.

She considered what needed to be done. "At least thirty minutes, but no more than an hour. Why don't you have some drinks at the bar and I'll let you know when everything is ready?"

"Perfect," I said with a smile. When Maude realized I was trying to make eye-contact, she smiled shyly and lowered her gaze. It suddenly occurred to me that Maude was a very attractive young lady and I wondered why I had never noticed before. Then I remembered Liz, turned, walked up behind her and wrapped my arms around her. "Honey, let's go have a few drinks and relax."

Liz reached behind and grabbed my ass. "Can't we go to our room first and check things out?"

As tempted as I was, Maude needed time to fix the room, so I had to distract Liz. Besides, I could always use a drink. "Oh, baby! Do behave." My Austin Powers impression wasn't very good, but it made her laugh. We took our bags and went to the bar. It wasn't far but to get there we had to go through a large open area with a grand piano on a round platform about fifteen feet across. The platform was layered in white marble. In fact, all the floors in the public areas of the hotel were tiled with various shades and colors of marble. Beyond the piano lounge and down six steps was the formal dining area. Beyond that and down another six steps was the main bar. Sure enough, Sam was at the bar serving drinks to a few guys who seemed to be having a great time. I helped Liz onto a stool and sat next to her.

Sam walked over with a smile. "How are you, Mr. Pierre? It's been a few months. Were you out of the country?"

I really didn't feel like talking about my neck. "No, nothing like that Sam, just busy with work."

Sam was still smiling politely. "So what can I get for you and the lovely lady?"

Another thing I liked about the Villa is that I didn't have a usual drink. When I was here, I made it a point to try mixed drinks with a tropical feel. "Well, I'll have a rum punch." I turned to Liz. "It's really good but Sam makes them strong."

Liz was shaking her head. "I don't want a rum punch." She turned to Sam, "Can I have a Piña Colada?"

Sam laughed, "Absolutely, and an excellent choice I might add." Then Sam turned to me, "A lovely woman who knows what she wants. Hang on to her sir."

I smiled at Sam, then turned to Liz and kissed her tenderly on the lips. "I have no intention of losing this one Sam. Liz here is the real deal."

For the next forty-five minutes, I entertained Liz with stories of my many adventures throughout different parts of Haïti until Sam interrupted, "I'm sorry sir, but you have a call at the front desk."

I thanked Sam and explained to Liz that it was probably the office, but I knew it was Maude. After excusing myself, I went to find out what she had been able to pull off. When I got to the front desk, I looked around to make sure Liz hadn't followed me, then leaned on the counter. "Okay Maude, what do you have for me?"

Maude was looking down at her notepad. "I was able to get two dozen roses and four assorted bouquets. I had housekeeping put a dozen roses on the bed, the other dozen roses are in a vase in the bathroom, and the assorted flowers were used to decorate the room. I also got you some candles. Please be careful; they are a fire hazard and are not allowed in the rooms, so please take them with you when you leave." Maude paused to make sure I understood the full meaning of what she had just said. The candles were a personal touch she added to help me out. "I inspected the room and everything is in order. All I need is your signature. I hope you don't mind the choice I made." She slid an envelope in front of me.

I assumed it was an invoice from the florist, but when I opened the envelope, inside it was a greeting card. On the front was a picture of a couple walking hand-in-hand down a beach and towards a beautiful sunset. Inside it was blank.

I was stunned. "Maude, this is perfect." I wrote in the card, To the most wonderful girl in the world. Thanks for showing me the meaning of happiness, and signed it.

Maude took the card, slipped it back into the envelope and called for a housekeeper. "I'm glad you approve Mr. Pierre. If you would give us just another minute or two, everything should be ready."

I wanted to hug her, but instead I extended my hand. "I don't even know how to thank you."

She took my hand and smiled, "Just doing my job Mr. Pierre." Then she suddenly pulled her hand away and looked down at her notes again. "I see your guest is looking for you."

As I turned, Liz was coming down the six peach-colored marble steps that led from the piano lounge to the main lobby and I walked towards her. "Baby, I'm sorry, it was the office, but I promise there will be no more interruptions."

Liz looked at me, then glanced at Maude with a suspicious look. "Are you sure it was the office?"

"Of course it was the office," I said. "No one else knows I'm here." I turned in time to see Maude hand the envelope to a house-keeper. I put my arms around Liz. "Baby, let's go finish our drinks so we can settle into our room."

Liz held me for a moment and then said, "Xavier, what was that woman saying to you?"

I led her towards the bar. "What woman?"

Liz stopped and looked at me, obviously annoyed. "Don't ask me 'what woman?' You know what woman, the woman at the front desk."

I gave her one of my sly smiles and put my arms around her again. "Oh her, she was just reminding me how lucky I am to be here with the most beautiful, [kiss] sexy, [kiss] gorgeous, [kiss] woman in the world." By now, my hands had moved down to her ass in a very public display of affection.

Liz knew we were in plain sight of the front desk. Reassured that her territory was properly marked, she smiled, "Okay baby, what-ever you say," and she kissed me. "Now let's go." Liz practically dragged me back to the bar and picked up her bag.

"Wait," I said, stalling for time. "Don't you want a snack?"

Liz grabbed my hand and started pulling. "The only thing I want to snack on right now is your nuts. Now baby please, get your bag and let's go to our room."

I started chuckling. "Honey, come on, my reputation is at stake here, how do you expect me to perform on an empty stomach?"

Liz was not amused but she knew how to get my attention. She let go of my hand, dropped her bag, and stood there while I backed up onto a stool. She then moved in between my legs and looked up into my eyes. "Okay baby, I've been waiting for a week and it hasn't killed me, so I suppose a few more minutes can't hurt." As she spoke, she started caressing my legs and working her way up. She licked her lips and looked down at my crotch. "But I suppose if you're gonna get a snack, I should get one too." By now, she had moved up and one hand was squeezing my semi-erect penis through my jeans while the other worked on my zipper. "You know, a little appetizer before the main course."

I checked out of the corner of my eye to make sure the three guys at the other end of the bar weren't looking our way. "Baby, I don't think we should be starting this here."

Satisfied she had made her point, Liz jumped on my comment. "No shit! Now baby can we please go to our room?"

Right about then a bellhop walked up to us. "Allow me to take your bags. Your room is ready."

"Yes!" Liz exclaimed, "Thank you so much!" She grabbed my hand and practically yanked me from the stool.

The bellhop carried our two small bags and led the way. Our room was on the far side of the pool, on the second floor. The wide hallways were all lined with works of art and the windows were decorated with wrought iron in the same intricate motifs. Inspired by the look of wonder on Liz' face, I leaned over and kissed her as we continued to follow the bellhop. I put my arm around her waist and smiled as she took it all in.

"This is beautiful," she said.

I nodded in agreement. "Only the best for my baby."

When we walked into the room it was beautiful. There were flowers on the nightstand, on the dresser, on top of the TV and on most other available surfaces. Also on the dresser was a bottle of champagne in a pewter ice bucket. And on the bed, a dozen long-stem roses, tied with a red ribbon. Liz was speechless. I gave the bellhop a tip and closed the door behind us. "Well, what do you think?"

Liz turned to me with a smile, "I think this is beautiful."

"Well, don't just stand there, get your roses," I prompted.

Liz was in a daze. She stepped towards the bed and noticed the card next to the roses. Instead of picking it up, she turned to me and said, "For me?"

A little confused, I nodded and said, "It's all for you."

Liz picked up the envelope and slowly opened it. After reading it, she held it to her heart and just stood there without saying a word.

I moved to hold her in my arms, "Darling, are you okay?"

Still holding the card to her heart, Liz said, "I'm better than okay. This is wonderful."

I decided not to say anything. I just held her close and rubbed her back.

After a while, Liz looked up at me. Her eyes were wet but she was smiling. "Xavier Pierre, Jr., I am so happy to have you in my life. I don't ever want to lose you."

I looked at Liz. "I don't know about that." I was suddenly struck with a feeling of great sadness and guilt. "I'm not the wonderful person you think I am." I couldn't even look her in the eyes anymore. "I've done a lot of things I'm not very proud of."

Suddenly, Liz wrapped her arms around me and squeezed hard. "I don't care about that. I love you, Xavier."

In the two weeks we had known each other neither of us had used the "L" word and I had promised myself that no matter what, I wouldn't use it that weekend. I even practiced a very reasonable, level-headed response in case she told me she loved me. I was supposed to tell her it was too soon to know how we felt. I was supposed to tell her we should take it slow and get to know each other before making those kinds of declarations. I had rehearsed it all. But before I knew it I heard myself saying, "I love you, Elizabeth." When I realized I had actually said it, there was a moment of panic. Then it sank in that I had just spoken to Liz from the heart. I took a deep breath and stepped back before looking into her eyes. "Yes, I love you. I really do." I leaned forward and kissed her. Before she could react I scooped her up and lay her on the bed and stepped away to light the candles. As I walked around the room lighting candles, I kept turning to her. She looked so tempting in her little summer dress. She kicked off her sandals and was about to unbutton her dress when I stopped her. "No. Don't do that. That's my job. I don't want you to do anything. Just lay back and enjoy."

When I had lit the last of the seven large white candles scattered around the room, I locked the door and turned out the lights. The mood was almost perfect. I grabbed the remote and put the TV on a smooth jazz music channel. Sade's silky voice filled the room with Sweetest Taboo. Standing at the foot of the bed, I kicked off my shoes and slowly unbuttoned my shirt while undressing Liz with my eyes. She started to fidget on the bed as she saw me looking at her. I took off the shirt and carelessly dropped it on the carpet as I approached her.

Kneeling at the foot of the bed, I held her feet. They were so beautiful. I kissed one, then the other. Liz moaned but she didn't pull her feet away. When I ran my tongue along the tips of her toes, they curled instantly. I kissed my way up the back of her left foot and gently licked her ankle until I could tell it was tickling her. Then I moved to the right ankle and kissed around to the heel of her foot. Then very slowly, I followed the edge of her right foot with my tongue. I started at the heel and left a glistening trail along the outer curve of her foot all the way to the little toe. Satisfied I had properly mapped the shape of her foot, I placed a delicate kiss on each toe. To give her calves the attention they deserved, I climbed up on the bed. I moved Liz' right leg so I could get between her calves, then I bent her left leg slightly so I could access the back of her calf. Starting at the heel of her foot, I licked a serpentine path up to the softness behind her knees.

When I kissed the space between the two tendons, Liz let out a cry "Xavier stop..." Then in a soft voice and with her eyes closed, "...you're killing me."

I ignored her and shifted my attention to her right leg. I kissed her kneecap as I ran my fingers softly up and down her right calf. At this point, Liz was moaning. Realizing that she could only take so much teasing I brought her knees together until she could feel my head between them. I wanted her to feel the warmth of my ears against her cool skin. I knew her eyes were closed so this was my way of announcing what I was about to do.

I let go of her knees and started kissing my way up the insides of her thighs. First, the left, then the right, a little higher each time, in a direct path that could only lead to one place. As I worked my way up, Liz spread her legs wider and wider to facilitate my advance as she chanted, "Yes... yes... yes..."

When I could go no further, I pressed my nose against her mound and inhaled her scent. Her panties were completely soaked. I worked my nose up und down her slit as if trying to shove the small patch of fabric inside her. The chanting stopped abruptly as Liz shouted, "Yes!" Then I got up off the bed and stood beside her. Liz opened her eyes and looked up at me. As she did, I unbuckled my belt, unzipped my jeans and let them fall to the carpet. Stepping out of my jeans, I pushed my briefs down to my ankles and stepped out of them.

Liz looked at my body. "Please Xavier, I can't wait anymore. Make love to me."

My erection disappeared from her sight as I knelt next to the bed and caressed her face with one hand as I slowly popped the buttons that ran down the entire length of her dress. When I got down to her tummy, I slid my hand inside her dress and traced two semi circles where the under wires of a bra would be if she were wearing one. "Isn't that what I'm doing?"

Her eyes closed again as she tried to be patient. "Yes, and it feels great. I can't wait to feel you inside me."

With a sudden movement my left hand was under the waistband of her panties and I slid two fingers into her wet hole. "Like this?"

Liz arched her back and turned her face away from me. "Oh god!" To get my fingers to go as deep as possible she braced her feet and pushed her pelvis up so only her feet, head, arms, and shoulders were on the bed.

Her reaction to my fingers was driving me crazy. I didn't know how much longer I could hold. I had to make her come soon or I would blow my load on the carpet. I leaned forward, clamped my mouth around her left nipple, pulled my two fingers out and shoved three fingers in.

In an instant, the transformation started. Up to now Liz had held back. She was, after all, my lady. But I didn't want a lady. I didn't want a girlfriend. I didn't even want a bitch, a whore or a slut. I wanted something much simpler, much dirtier and she gave me exactly what I wanted. A massive orgasm pushed her over the edge as she screamed out in ecstasy, "Oh shit! You bastard! You fucking bastard! Oh god, I love you!" She knew that she had been changed. She had become my property.

Satisfied with the transformation, I climbed on top of her and started kissing her neck very tenderly as she struggled to catch her breath. When I started kissing her lips, the smell of her juices still fresh on my face compelled her to lick my mouth and nose with broad strokes of her tongue. She was like an animal in heat and I loved her all the more for it. My heart was racing as I realized I would do anything for this woman. I had only been this much in love once before and that had been with Alice.

I couldn't put it off any longer; I had to have her. I jumped off the bed and started searching through my bag. Liz propped herself up on her elbows, curious to see what I was up to. "Baby, what are you doing?"

When I found the box of condoms, I held it up for her to see. "Just getting these."

Her face lit up with a greedy look as she realized what was next. Liz lay back, spread her legs and started to play with herself, as she spoke to me. "Oh baby, come give me my cock. You know I'm yours, right? Come fuck your pussy. Fuck me good baby. I need you to fuck me nice and hard."

I needed no prompting. With a quick motion, I put on a condom and knelt between her knees. It had taken all my strength to wait this long, but the moment had finally come and I wanted nothing between me and what was now rightfully mine. Without saying a word, I grabbed Liz' left ankle and passed it over my head. As I did, I slipped a hand under her ass and flipped her over. She immediately understood and went on all fours. I grabbed her by the hips and moved my penis into position. "How did you say you want it?"

Instead of answering, Liz put her head on the bed and reached between her legs. With one hand, she pulled the crotch of her g-string to the side. With the other, she grabbed my shaft and guided the head towards her waiting hole. Once my head was past her outer lips she released my shaft and slammed back into me.

"Fuck!" I yelled. I grabbed her hips and began to thrust against her as she bucked liked a woman possessed. I would have come by the third stroke, but we were out of sync. Liz had completely lost control and was grunting like a wild animal. She was having another orgasm. As she came down from her climax, she started to move forward and back with a steady rhythm. "Don't stop! Fuck me! Please give it all to me!"

I was way ahead of her. "I won't stop even if you beg me to!" With both hands on her hips, I matched her rhythm, thrusting forward everytime she slammed back. Soon it was my turn to cry out in ecstasy. Liz came right along with me. As she had her third orgasm, a tremor went through my body like a bolt of lightning only to be followed by a second, then a third. Finally, my strength spent, I collapsed on top of Liz. Maybe it was the week of anticipation. Maybe it was the love I felt for Liz. Or maybe it was both, but I had just had what could only be described as an earth-shattering orgasm and we were only an hour into the weekend!

I tried to move so as to shift my weight off Liz' back but she protested by clenching her inner muscles. "Don't take it out. Just hold me."

I rolled us onto our sides so that she would be more comfortable and wrapped my arms around her. I was still stiff inside her, but my strength was exhausted. Liz lay almost motionless but I felt her inner muscles clenching and relaxing and she was moaning very softly. As tired as I was, the thought that she was about to have a fourth orgasm excited my already stiff cock back to a full erection. While still on my side, I started making small circular motions with my hips. It was all I had the strength to do but apparently it was enough.

The moaning got louder until Liz exclaimed, "I don't believe this!" I held her tight as she had her fourth climax. When she was finally still, I pulled out, rolled onto my back, and pulled her on top of me. Soon we were asleep.

I have no idea how many times we made love, but it just seemed like one long session lasting all weekend. From that point, our relationship moved along rapidly. I had found love again. I spent as much time as possible with Liz. I put Yasmine on notice that she was no longer welcome to spend weekends with me and my all-night benders at the Flamenco came to a halt. I would stop by once or twice a week, but it was to eat, not to hang out. I still drank, but it was under control. I wanted to be a good man and treat Liz like the lady she was. Days turned into weeks, weeks turned into months, and everything seemed to be going fine. I was as happy as I could be under the circumstances. And despite the secrets I kept in my heart, I dared believe I could live a normal life. I dared believe I could love.

Chapter 9
"Summer Vacation"

The first two months with Liz were great but I could already feel the passion starting to dwindle. The first clue was I had very little interest in the small things that made up her day. I pretended to care, but more than once she got upset because she was telling me something that was of great importance to her, only to realize I wasn't paying attention. Also, I was spending more time at the Flamenco and I was drinking more.

One day, I sat in my office trying to do work, but my mind kept drifting to Nicole. She was on my mind a lot and that was yet another clue. Finally, I stopped fighting it and abandoned myself to the fantasy. Nicole was standing naked in front of me, doing her best to avoid my eyes. Her genuine shyness and modesty, despite her obvious beauty, were two of the things that had always attracted me to her. As I pulled her towards me, I could almost feel the palms of my hands cupping the twin globes of that delicious ass of hers; her dual mounds of chocolate sweetness driving me crazy as I drew her in closer still. Slowly, I guided my shaft between her legs. Inch by inch, I pushed the head closer and closer to her wet pussy until I was ready to enter. Then...

"Xavier... Xavier..."

Startled, I turned my head to see my assistant peeking her head inside my doorway. "Yes, Olivia."

I had no idea how long Olivia had been standing there. She looked at me with a curious look, then said, "Sorry to disturb you boss, but I was wondering if I could leave early today. I have to pick up my son from the infirmary."

I smiled at her, "Of course." After a moment, I realized what she had just said and frowned. "Is your son okay?"

"He's fine," she said. "Just a cold but the school asked me to pick him up early."

At that point, I wanted to say, "Why can't your good-for-nothing husband get his out-of-work ass off the damn couch and go pick up his son?" But instead, I just said "Okay, I hope he feels better."

After Olivia left, I stopped to take stock of the situation. I had a girlfriend who was intelligent, beautiful, sexy, had class and was great in bed, yet I couldn't stop thinking of another girl that I knew for a fact I wasn't in love with. That just didn't make any sense. Especially if I was in love with Liz. I mean I was in love with her, right?

The realization I might not be in love was very sobering. What the hell was my problem? It had felt so real and so strong. People don't just fall out of love after a couple of months... do they?

I tried to reassure myself it was probably some primitive fear of commitment rooted deep inside my inner brain. As much as that sounded like some touchy-feely crap from a self-help infomercial, I needed something to hang onto. The thought I might be completely incapable of feeling true love for a woman scared me beyond description. I had to love Liz. In fact, I was going to prove that I loved her. I pushed Nicole out of my mind and thought of a plan.

In the four years I had worked at The Agency, I had never taken a vacation. I generally used my vacation days to take long weekends, but even then, I often stopped by the office for a couple of hours before heading out to the beach. I needed a real vacation. I needed to get away from it all: clear my mind, step back and get a perspective on my life. I knew the only way I would get a real vacation was to leave the country. The way I figured it, time away from Liz would give me an opportunity to miss her, and missing her would prove that I loved her because I never missed anyone.

Okay, my decision was made. All I needed to do was make a few phone calls. First I called Florence, the Human Resources Co-ordinator, and found that despite my taking a long weekend every couple of months, I had eighteen days in the vacation bank. That was almost enough for a four-week vacation. I decided to put in a request for three weeks and save a few days so I could take some long weekends with Liz when I got back. Next, I called my mother. I didn't talk to Mom much, maybe once every few months. There were so many things we didn't see eye-to-eye on, the most important being Alice. Of course, Mom had been mostly right about my ex-wife, but I certainly wasn't going to admit that to her. But we had finally come to an understanding, and I had moved back home to keep Pop company. When I thought about being with my mother for three weeks, I started having second thoughts. Maybe it wasn't such a good idea after all. I considered another option. I could stay at my father's house on Long Island, but that would be worse than staying with Mom. I had to call before I changed my mind about the whole vacation. I dialed the number and entered my international access code.

"Hello, Pouchon, is everything okay?" The worry in my mother's voice was unmistakable.

I couldn't help getting annoyed, "Mom, why do you have to assume that because I'm calling something has to be wrong?"

"Because you never call your mother," she snapped. "What's wrong? Is Pop okay?"

"Mom, Pop is fine."

"What about the house?" she interrupted, "Please tell me my plants are okay. Has the gardener been coming?"

I had no idea if the gardener had been coming or not: everything looked relatively green so I assumed it was okay. "Mom, will you please stop worrying, everything is fine."

"Then why are you calling? You never call. Do you have any idea how it makes me feel that my son never calls me?"

I was starting to think that going to New Jersey was a bad idea. I hadn't even bought the ticket and Mom and I were arguing. "Mom, if you'd let me talk, I would tell you."

Mom was on a roll. "Well, if you would get to the point instead of beating around the bush all the time."

I put my head down on my desk with a sigh. "I wanna come up to New Jersey."

With hardly a pause, Mom was off again. "What do you mean? Oh my god, what did you do? Did you get fired?"

I knew it wasn't her intention to upset me, but Mom had a way of disturbing my inner peace without even trying. But I have to admit, I also knew how to get under her skin, and when I did, it was always on purpose. "Mom, please! I'm taking three weeks off and I just wanted to visit, but if that's too much to ask, forget it. I'll just go to the Dominican Republic," then after a pause, "or maybe I'll just fly out to Long Island and spend some time with Dad."

Mom definitely felt that one. "Your dad? Why would you do such a thing? And why are you putting words in my mouth? You know you can stay with me. Besides, there's no room at your father's house."

I could tell she was hurt, but I was too angry to apologize or stop my subtle attack. "Well, if it's not too much trouble, I suppose I can stay with you."

Mom just sighed and said, "When are you coming?"

"I'm not sure," I said, "maybe next week. I haven't even told Pop yet."

"Okay," she said, "call me as soon as you know, so I can plan on picking you up. Make sure you land in Newark."

This was exactly the kind of crap that really pissed me off. Less than a minute after I told her I was coming, and she was already changing my plans. "You don't have to pick me up. I'm landing at Kennedy Airport and I'm renting a car."

"Why would you want to rent a car?" Mom was relentless. "Use my car."

"Mom, I want to have fun. Sharing a car with you is not my idea of fun."

"You won't have to share," she said, "I get a car at work. I don't use mine anymore."

"Okay," I said, "let me think about that."

"There's nothing to think about!" she shouted. "You're staying with me and you're using my car."

"Why are you yelling?" I shouted back. "If I want to get yelled at, there are plenty of local numbers I can call instead of paying to make this international call."

"I'm not yelling!" she shouted again. "Why is it that every time I open my mouth you accuse me of yelling?"

"Because you are always yelling," I said. "Anyway, I'm at work so I can't stay. I'll call you with my itinerary."

Sensing I was on the edge, Mom softened her voice. "Tell Pop to pay the gardener. He's supposed to come every week. I paid a fortune for those flowers and plants, you know."

"Yes Mom, I'll tell him."

"Pouchon…"

"Yes, Mom."

"...I love you."

"I love you too Mom."

After I hung up, I tried to look at the bright side. Staying with Mom meant no hotel and no car to rent, and that meant more money for booze and partying. Not a bad deal. Next question was the date. It would have to be after the next payday. I made very good money but I had no savings. I spent money as fast I could make it, often faster. Saving money just didn't make sense when I had just about everything I wanted and I could have anything else just by signing my name. Besides, I had nothing to save for.

I looked at the calendar and fired off a memo to administration requesting tickets leaving for New York the following Friday and returning three weeks later.

That night, I told Pop about my vacation plans. His reaction was positive but not enthusiastic. Next, I had to tell Liz. I called her to tell her I would be taking a three-week vacation to visit family in the States. That didn't go over as well as I expected. After a long silence, she started grilling me with questions like, "How could you decide this without me?" and "How could you be so selfish?" and "Did you ever stop to consider how this would affect me?"

I just listened quietly. She obviously didn't realize I was taking this trip for her. Well, for us. I mean, of course I was expecting to have fun, but I was doing it to get us closer. But of course she couldn't see that. Women could be so self-centered.

Nevertheless, I made it a point to spend extra time with her, and reassured her the majority of my time would be spent visiting specialists for my neck and attending to family business. She couldn't understand why that would take three weeks, but I addressed all her objections the same way. I wrapped my arms around her, kissed her neck and gently caressed her back. Liz was such a sensual woman. It seemed as though she was never more than a caress away from arousal and I never failed to use that to my advantage and our mutual pleasure.

When the day came to travel to New York, a driver from the office came to pick me up. I kissed Pop and Mary, and gave Nelson a hug. He wanted to escort me to the airport but I told him that wasn't necessary. With the 'International Agency' plates, my driver would be able to drive past the security barrier and drop me off closer to the terminal without airport police bothering us. I would get V.I.P. treatment right up until the moment I cleared customs. Once I got on the plane I was just an ordinary guy flying coach, but that was okay. The instant the plane left the ground I was as good as in the U.S.

Later, as the plane leveled off, I closed my eyes and started to drift off. Not quite asleep, I thought about a very different flight I had been on many years earlier.

∞:∞

"What's your name?" she asked.

"Xavier," I answered politely.

"That's a very nice name," she said.

"Thank you," I replied.

"Would you like something to drink?" she asked.

I wasn't thirsty, but I hoped that if I gave her something to do, she would leave me alone. "Okay, can I have some soda please?"

"You certainly can," she said with a smile.

The stewardess was extremely kind but soon wanted to know all about me. It was 1978 and I guess it wasn't every day she saw a 14-year old kid, by himself, in the first-class lounge en route to Spain. My father was sleeping comfortably in his seat downstairs. It was the first and last time he and I traveled together alone. I think the idea was to get my father and me to bond. I wanted to see the lounge so I went up the spiral staircase. A minute later, a stewardess was dispatched to attend to my needs. I had been on lots of airplanes but this was different. This was first-class on a 747. I had never begged for anything before, but I begged my mother to upgrade us to first-class. After discussing it with my father, she consented and paid for the upgrade.

As I stared out the window into the blackness of night, the stewardess continued to ask her questions about my family and what they did for a living. When I told her that my mom worked for Trans World Airlines, she said "Oooooh, I see!" In her mind, the mystery was solved. It would be another three hours before we landed in Madrid, Spain. Didn't she have other passengers to look after? I guessed not, since most of them were sleeping.

My father and I spent three days in Spain and seven days in Italy. The trip was memorable for many reasons: the picture I took in front of the Roman Coliseum; seeing Pope John Paul I before he died so soon after becoming Pope; looking up at the ceiling of the Sistine Chapel; and let's not forget drinking real sangria in Spain while watching authentic flamenco dancers.

❧:❧

"Chicken or beef?" the stewardess asked.

I opened my eyes and looked at her. "Beef please, and let me have a Heineken with that." This wasn't first class and I wasn't on my way to Europe, but at least they were still serving meals on flights more than four hours. It had been several years since I had been home. I had been in Miami earlier that year for business, but that didn't count. Miami didn't even feel like part of America. No, this time I was really going home. Despite my mother's insistence, I would be landing at JFK airport. From there, I would take the train across the Hudson River, then a New Jersey Transit train to Summit, NJ. My mother lived just a few minutes from the train station. When she came to pick me up, we were very glad to see each other. She looked good. She looked happy. We went back to her apartment and had dinner. After that I went to the store for beer and spent the night getting drunk in front of the TV.

The next morning the sweet smells of cinnamon, freshly cut grass and fabric softener filled my nostrils. Convinced I must be dreaming, I rolled over on the soft cotton sheets as a lawn mower droned in the distance. "At least this is a nice dream," I thought to myself as I drifted back to sleep. Sometime later I opened my eyes and wondered at the room I was in. The ceiling was full of odd slopes and angles. My bed was nestled in an alcove and the window behind the low headboard was framed with a heavy curtain held open with thick gold ropes. The multiple layers were in various shades and textures of burgundy. Behind that harmonious blend of satin, linen and velvet, a thin white curtain decorated with lace and embroidered with white flowers provided just the right amount of shade while letting daylight fill the room. I sat up in the bed and looked around. I could hear my mother's voice echoing in the hallway outside and I remembered where I was.

Later that day we drove to Marymount College to see my sister who was spending the summer on campus. It was great seeing her. Even though I was eight years older, we had been very close growing up. For several years, I was the father figure in her life, and she always wanted to be where I was. I loved her dearly and as much as possible I let her hang out with my friends and me. My main concern was that I didn't want her exposed to drugs. Other than that, I allowed her in our company as we drank, smoked cigarettes, and joked around on the front porch. I even allowed her to take a few sips of whatever I was drinking. Of course, getting her to finally go to bed was always a challenge as she begged to stay with us a bit longer. And keeping her so close to my inner circle meant that she always had a crush on one of my friends, but she was a great kid and always did exactly what I told her, so her infatuations were no cause for concern.

When I was about sixteen and my sister was eight, Mom rented a house in downtown Port-au-Prince, on 2nd Jeremy Street. Mom hired a governess so we would have adult supervision. Mrs. Dejean was a very kind old lady, but it was soon clear I wasn't just the man of the house, but the one in charge. She deferred to me in all matters of any importance. All she did was supervise the other staff. Incredibly, even in that small house, we had a staff of four. The governess; a housekeeper who cooked, cleaned and did my laundry; a yard boy who maintained the yard and did the mopping in the house; and last, but not least, a second maid whose primary function was to care for my sister. She would dress my sister, comb her hair, wash her clothes and walk her to school. Now that was a sight, seeing my eight year old sister walking to school, accompanied by a uniformed maid who carried her book bag and held a parasol over her head to shelter her from the sun! Ridiculous, but that was how our Mom wanted things to be, so that's how things were. But I was the one who made sure Sis did her homework. I administered all discipline, including corporal punishment. I was the parent if her school requested a meeting or a signature. And I was the one the governess and the maids threatened to report her to when she misbehaved.

I assumed I would always be there to protect and guide my sister until she married someone who met with my approval, and she probably assumed the same. But life had different plans. When she was only thirteen, I had a terrible car accident and she didn't see me again for four years. When I finally moved back to Haïti, my mother, stepfather and sister were living in our new house at Delmas 75. I had really hoped that my sister and I could pick up where we left off, but I had been gone too long. I wasn't there during some of the most traumatic events of her life. To make matters worse and against my advice, a few months after I moved back, my sister moved to our father's house on Long Island. I warned her that living with our father wouldn't be easy, but she was determined to do it her way, so I gave my blessing and some pointers on dealing with the old man.

Despite my premonitions, no one could have predicted that

staying with our father would have turned into such a disaster. Surprisingly, the real problem turned out to be my father's new wife. Although twenty-two years younger than my father, Josie was a wonderful woman and I loved her very much, but my sister was a rebellious teenager and the two of them just couldn't get along. My sister escaped by enrolling in Marymount.

The campus was nice enough, but almost empty; not surprising since it was summer. As my sister took me for a tour, I realized that she wasn't a kid anymore. We talked about everything I had missed while she had been in Haïti without me. I felt somehow responsible that she had to go through her struggles alone. We talked for hours until Sis changed the subject. "Tomorrow you'll meet Daisy."

"Who the heck is Daisy?" I asked.

"A friend from grade school," she answered.

I racked my brain but the name didn't ring a bell. "I don't remember a Daisy."

My sister smiled as we approached her dorm room. "You don't know her. She and I became friends after your accident."

"Is she hot?" I asked as my sister inserted her key in the lock.

Sis stopped in her tracks. "What do you mean, hot?"

Oblivious to the hint of anger in her voice, I proceeded to define hot. "You know, nice ass, big tits."

I had barely spoken the words when my sister grabbed me by the collar with both hands and pushed me against the wall. "Don't even think about it. I swear Pouchon, Daisy is my best friend. You touch her and I'll kill you!"

Taken aback, I said, "Hey Sis, relax. It was just a question."

"Don't give me that shit, Pouchon," my sister insisted, "I know you."

Remembering the reason for this vacation, I reassured her. "Don't worry, Poupette, I have a girlfriend. All I'm looking for is innocent fun. You know, rest and relaxation."

I was smiling my devilish grin, as Sis let go of me. I think she had even surprised herself with her outburst, but she wasn't done yet. As she let us in her room she continued, "I'm serious Pouchon, Daisy is very innocent."

I laughed out loud. "Oh please, give me a break. Who is she, Little Red Riding Hood? And who am I, the big bad wolf?"

"Stop making fun," my sister said. "She's a virgin."

My mouth almost dropped open. "Oh hell no! They still make those?"

Sis punched my arm. "Knock it off. And whatever you do, don't tell her I told you."

"Puh-lease," I said in a mocking tone, "you don't need to worry about your friend, I don't mess with virgins."

My sister's room was a typical dorm room. She had a poster on the door but mostly it reflected the tastes of a young woman entering adulthood on a budget. One picture caught and kept my attention. Above her bed, my sister had a photograph of a young couple on a bed. The young woman was very pretty and wore a sexy, pink baby-doll with matching panties. She was leaning against the headboard with her long legs extended out in front of her. The young man wore loose fitting black jeans and no shirt. He sat crossed-legged with the girl's feet in his lap. In his left hand, he held one of the girl's feet as he carefully applied pink polish to her toes with his other hand. The girl's head was tilted back and she had a dreamy look in her eyes. The boy had a knowing grin on his face. I liked the photo instantly. That night, my sister took me around campus and introduced me to some of her girlfriends. We both had lots of beer, but for the most part I was on my best behavior.

The next day, Mom picked us up and we drove to our aunt's house in Brooklyn. We would be spending the weekend there for easier access to Manhattan nightlife. Daisy joined us later in the afternoon; she would be spending the weekend with us.

The instant I saw Daisy I was shocked. Even though she was twenty-one, she looked closer to thirteen. She was only five feet tall and had the round face of a child. It was only after a bit that I realized that she had rather large breasts and a very nice, round ass. There was something very obscene about the way she was put together. She looked liked a very fuckable little girl. Of course, the tight jeans and flirty top only made it worse. I gave myself a mental slap and reminded myself that I didn't do virgins. But I couldn't shake the attraction quite so easily. It was hard to believe no one had popped her cherry. Even as I stared at her, she seemed oblivious to the fact I was checking her out. Daisy extended her hand with a childlike smile. "Hi, my name is Daisy."

I accepted her hand and pulled her into my arms. As I gave her a warm hug, I said, "Pleased to meet you Daisy. My sister has told me a lot about you." Then I kissed her on the cheek.

"She told me a lot about you as well," Daisy replied in a high-pitched childlike voice that matched her face. I couldn't help noticing she seemed genuinely excited to meet me.

That night we went barhopping in Manhattan. Sis and Daisy were both looking really hot with their heels, mini-skirts and skimpy tops. Dressed like that and with a little makeup, Daisy managed to look about eighteen. I decided it was best if I ignored her. She was a virgin and she was my sister's best friend. That was about as untouchable as a girl could get but Daisy wasn't about to make it easy for me to ignore her. The entire night she focused all her attention on me.

The next day, Mom dragged us out to Long Island to see our father. My sister hated the idea, but she hadn't seen Dad in quite some time so she didn't say a word. Daisy was coming along, so my sister probably hoped that would curb my father's tongue. Dad could be a real jerk sometimes but he was always perfectly charming in the presence of strangers.

Visiting Dad worked out well enough. Seeing him was nice and there were no incidents. On the way back, Mom took us on an evening Soca cruise. The cruise was one big floating Caribbean party, and I got to indulge in my appetite for alcohol. I was dodging Daisy all night in order to drink. Every time I bought a drink, I would guzzle half before anyone saw me, so it looked like I was nursing the same drink all night long. By the time we headed back home I was drunk. Turned out my sister was pretty toasted as well. Normally, I had no hesitation to drive drunk. I even had a theory that a sure-fire way to sober up quickly was to get behind the wheel of a car. But I didn't feel like driving. Besides, I had something a lot more fun in mind.

I told my mom I was feeling kind of sleepy and asked if she wouldn't mind driving, then I got in the back seat. Normally, Sis would have sat in the back with Daisy but she couldn't very well leave Mom up front by herself, so she rode shotgun by default. Once we were on our way, I settled back and pretended to sleep. Soon, my sister was gently snoring up front.

Daisy, not having had any alcohol to drink, was wide awake and visibly bored. Sensing that the time was right, I reached out and carefully found her hand. Out of the corner of my eye, I could see her smile when I gave her hand a gentle squeeze. She squeezed back and held my hand in both of hers. Content to go no further, Daisy leaned back and closed her eyes, still smiling. I had other ideas. Pretending to get more comfortable, I put a sweater over our laps so that our hands were invisible. Next, I pried my hand from between hers and put it on her thigh. All the way back to Mom's house, I caressed and teased, inching closer and closer to her panties with each pass. I was hoping to go further but she wouldn't spread her legs. A part of me was excited by the challenge, but another part of me was grateful that she wasn't giving in to me and hoped that she never would.

Even in my drunken state, I knew I should leave Daisy alone, but I rationalized that it was her fault; she was the one who had tempted me beyond my ability to resist. The truth was that I found her very attractive. There was something about her innocence that really turned me on and made me want to fuck her brains out. When we got home, I argued with my sister about where Daisy should sleep. Too drunk to care about what was appropriate or not, I insisted that Daisy sleep with me and even tried to convince her that I would be a perfect gentleman if she agreed to share my bed. Despite my efforts, and in frustration, I went to bed alone.

The following day, Daisy had to go back to her aunt's house in Brooklyn. After scolding me for acting like a fool the night before, she gave me her phone number and made me promise to call. And I did. In fact, I called every night that we weren't together. During one of our talks, I asked her if she had ever been in my sister's dorm room. She said yes, so I asked her to visualize the room. When I asked if she remembered the photograph of the young couple in bed, Daisy giggled as she told me she could see it clearly. Then I had her imagine that it was us. "Can you see me holding your foot?" I asked.

"Yes," she said.

"But I would put the polish on last," I said. "First, I would give you a foot massage. Have you ever had a foot massage?"

"No," she replied with another giggle.

"Well, I'll have to give you one. Of course, I'll have to nibble on your toes just a little bit," I teased in a deep voice.

"No! You can't do that," she exclaimed. "I'm ticklish."

I laughed. "You have sensitive feet. I like that. Where else are you sensitive?"

"I'm not telling you," she said, still giggling.

"Works for me," I said, "more fun finding out for myself. Should I start with your feet and work my way up, or should I start kissing on your neck and work my way down?"

And so, it continued every night, into the early hours of the morning. More intoxicating than any drug, her innocence drew me in like a trap. Even as I titillated her senses and teased her mind, the fact she had no clue of the effect she was having on me made our conversations all the more stimulating, but I needed more. It was time for a face-to-face meeting, but I had to be careful and keep things innocent. I had to make her want me without touching her. But where was the fun in that?

Okay, what if I could only touch her hands? I smiled to myself. Perfect, that should present an interesting challenge while making sure it didn't get out of control.

I got my opportunity a few days later. I called Daisy and told her I wanted to see her alone. I was dropping my sister on campus, I'd have the car and no one would be expecting me for hours. Daisy was stuck at home because she had no ride, but she would be alone for several hours late in the afternoon. It was perfect, but Daisy had a concern. "Xavier, there's something I haven't told you about me. I don't really want to tell you, but I guess I should."

I reassured her, "Sweetie, trust me, nothing you tell me will make me think any less of you. Just think of all the things we've shared since we met. Who could have predicted that we would have gotten so close?"

"You are so right," she said, "I feel very close to you. I've told you stuff your own sister doesn't know, and she's my best friend."

I had spent countless late-night hours making her feel comfortable and winning her trust. That investment was about to pay off. "Well, I've told you plenty that Sis doesn't know about me either. I'm normally a very private person, but with you it's different, it just feels so natural. Do you know what I mean?"

"Yes I do," she said. "It does feel natural." She paused a moment. I could sense her coming to a decision. The outcome was certain so I waited patiently for her to accept the inevitable. Then she spoke, "Well, it's just something that I don't want guys to know but..." she took a deep breath, "...I'm still a virgin."

I didn't say a word, intentionally building up the tension.

The anxiety in Daisy's voice was palpable, "Xavier, please say something?"

I let her off the hook, "I'm sorry honey, I was waiting for you to finish."

"I am finished," she said.

"Okay," I started, "Daisy, I'm not sure why you're telling me this. I think it has to do with my behavior the night you slept over in New Jersey. I'm really embarrassed about that. Being drunk is a poor excuse for acting like a fool but it's the only explanation I have. Please forgive me."

"Oh no!" she said, "It's not that. I just didn't want you to come over and think... I mean I wouldn't want to give the impression that..."

As she fumbled for a graceful exit that didn't exist, I rescued her. "Daisy, when I come over, absolutely nothing will happen that you aren't completely comfortable with. Not only are you my sister's best friend, but I would hate to do anything to make you think less of me.

"I really appreciate that," she said. "I can't wait to see you Xavier."

I could actually hear the smile in her voice and it made me smile as well in anticipation of what was to come.

On the way to her aunt's house, I stopped at a liquor store and bought a bottle of cheap vodka and some double-mint gum. I hated vodka but, along with being high in alcohol, vodka had a very important property: minimal alcohol breath. The gum was to make absolutely sure. When I got to the building, the bottle was down to three quarters. Daisy buzzed me in and I went up to the fourth floor apartment.

"Sorry I took so long," I said. "I had to make a stop on the way and pick up something for my mother. If I had forgotten, she would have killed me."

"It's okay," she said, "the only thing is that my aunt will be here in less than an hour and you can't be here when she comes home." Daisy led me to the couch. "I'm sorry. I thought she'd be out longer."

"It's okay," I said. Daisy was wearing a pair of tight black shorts and a t-shirt that would have been fairly loose if her breasts weren't so full. And with the little slippers she wore on her tiny feet, she looked absolutely delicious. Reminding myself that I could only touch her hands, I swallowed hard and closed my eyes to get my focus.

"You okay?" Daisy asked.

"Fine," I said as I opened my eyes with a smile, "but I have to say, you look good enough to eat."

Daisy giggled. "Stop it, you're embarrassing me."

Realizing that time was short, I reached out and took her hand.

As I did, I squeezed it gently and smiled at her. "It's true, you have very sexy legs and please forgive me for saying this, but you have the most kissable lips I've ever seen."

"Stop," she said, "you promised to be good."

I could tell from the huge smile that every word was making her warm inside. "I made no such promise. What I said was that nothing would happen that you weren't comfortable with. I didn't say a damn thing about being good." Still caressing her hand as I spoke, I winked at her. She turned away and as she did, I brought her hand to my mouth and kissed the back of it. I made it a wet kiss. "Delicious, I really could eat you."

Daisy turned to face me and said, "Oh damn."

I could see she was breathing heavily and I looked into her eyes. "Are you okay?"

"I'm fine," she answered, "I just wasn't expecting that."

"No man has ever kissed your hand before?" I asked.

"Not like that," she answered.

I turned her hand so the palm was up and slowly ran my fingers across her small palm and down her tiny fingers. "Your hands are so soft. I can just imagine how they would feel against my skin." Without waiting for a response, I brought her hand to my face and ran the back of it against my cheek, as I looked deep into her eyes.

Daisy said nothing as she tried to keep up with the cascade of words and sensations I was sending her way. Still maintaining eye contact, I moved her hand to my mouth and raked the tip of my tongue gently and slowly across her fingertips. Daisy's mouth opened but no words came out. As I started to suck on her fingertips, one at a time, and very slowly, Daisy's eyelids dropped until her eyes closed completely. From the smile on her face, I knew she was enjoying the stimulation. When I ran her fingertips across the edge of my teeth, she gasped. Her eyes were still closed as I nibbled on her fingertips. "You sure you okay hon?" I asked coyly.

Daisy let out a heavy sigh. "I've never felt anything like this before."

While caressing the back of her hand, I started kissing her knuckles. "It's hard to believe no one has ever taken the time to kiss these hands before." I said.

"Not like this," she repeated.

"How sad," I said. "If these hands were in my care, I would make sure they were never neglected." I straightened out her index and middle fingers and curled her other fingers into her palm so that she was making an upside down peace sign. "But trust me, I would treat the rest of your body right too." As I looked at her tiny feet, shapely calves, and sexy thighs, I licked her fingertips again and said, "I would suck your toes." I dotted the tip of my tongue up both fingers. "I would kiss your legs." I kissed the last phalanges of both fingers, just below the palms. "I would take extra time on your thighs, then who knows what I would do." As I spoke the words, I flicked my tongue across the skin between her fingers. Daisy jumped noticeably but I just turned up the intensity, locking my lips on that small triangle of skin between her fingers and sucking gently.

Daisy started to pull her hand away but I held fast. "Xavier... oh god, please stop... Xavier, you have to go."

I took her hand away from my mouth but continued to hold it. "What's wrong?"

Daisy was still breathing quickly and she sounded nervous. "Nothing's wrong, I just don't want us to get caught."

I tried not to laugh but I couldn't suppress a huge grin, "Caught doing what, kissing your hand?"

Daisy was clearly flustered. "Well no, I mean yes, I mean I'm sorry. I'm not sure what I'm trying to say, but I know you have to go."

"Daisy, what's wrong?" I asked, trying not to smile.

Daisy stood up and pulled me from the couch. "Please Xavier, just go." She ushered me to the door and as I was leaving, she kissed me on the cheek. "Xavier, I'm so sorry to make you go like this, but I'm really glad you came. Please call me as soon as you get home so I know you're safe."

I waited until I got to my car to laugh. After driving a few blocks, I pulled over and took a swig of vodka (one for the road) before finding my way back to the highway.

The day came to see a specialist about my neck. X-rays revealed that I had done severe and permanent damage to vertebrae four and five. An interesting coincidence was Christopher Reeves fell off a horse and broke his neck a week before me. When I mentioned this to the doctor in casual conversation, he told me he was professionally acquainted with the doctors who were treating Mr. Reeves. When I asked if Reeves would ever walk again, the doctor simply shook his head.

Reading my thoughts, he said, "You're a very lucky man, Xavier. You could easily be sharing Mr. Reeves' fate. As it is, you'll have pain on and off the rest of your life, but nothing you can't manage. Of course, that may change in your later years."

Between my high tolerance for physical pain and my conviction that I wouldn't make it to old age, the news was actually quite good. I thanked the doctor and left.

My last weekend in the States, Daisy joined Sis and I as we went to Manhattan. Sis had told us about a club called Nell's that was supposed to be great. When we got there, the place was jumping. It was everything Sis said it would be, and more. Scores of us were going deaf as the bass-heavy rhythms thundered from the massive speakers. Private planets collided as each patron grooved to the shared oblivion of sound, substance and sex. The sound was a mix of everything from the 80s, top 40, hip-hop and R&B. But regardless of the type of track being played, the driving base line was inalterable. The substance was a blend of alcohol flowing liberally at all the bars, and the illicit drugs for sale in the bathrooms. Few cravings were left unsatisfied. And the sex? It was everywhere, as scantily clad women of all shapes, sizes, and shades competed for my attention. Deciding I was best suited to rule this happy universe, I shouted at the top of my lungs, "The roof, the roof!" and without missing a beat, a hundred voices responded around me, "The roof is on fire!" And all together we chanted, "We don't need no water, let the motherfucker burn! Burn motherfucker, burn!" Satisfied that my subjects were content under my rule I danced among them. We all danced. There were no pairs. We all danced together. I had achieved peace on earth and brotherly love. In a vain attempt to cement these bonds more permanently I yelled again, "The roof, the roof!" The reaction was even more thunderous now that everyone knew what was expected. Even the few wallflowers joined, not only in the chant, but they came forward. A power greater than them had called them to the dance floor.

Sis and Daisy were dancing at the opposite end of the dance floor. Looking out at the crowd, I could see a young woman standing next to one of the large columns at the edge of the dance floor. She was pretty and wore a blue dress that went down just below her knees. Not only was she showing far less skin than any other girl, but, more importantly, she wasn't dancing. I had to talk to her.

Now that she had caught my attention, I had to catch hers. It didn't take long before she looked my way. When she did, I held her gaze until she smiled and turned away. I strode across the dance floor in time with the beat, slipped around the column and tapped her on the shoulder from behind. Surprised, she whirled around. Smiling enthusiastically, I took her by the hand and started to pull her towards the dance floor and shouted, "Come on, I know you can dance!"

"Oh no!" she said, "I'm not very good."

I ignored her and continued smiling and pulling her into the crowd of dancers. "Just let yourself go. Feel the music inside you!"

Reluctantly, she started first to move, then to dance. As she did, I looked her over and tried to imagine where she was from. I was guessing she had probably come from a wedding. In any case, there was only one way to find out. After a few tracks, I took her by the hand and led her off the dance floor. "Let's go upstairs," I said.

One of the nice things about Nell's is that it was three clubs in one. The first floor featured dance music, the second floor had reggae and the third floor was a jazz club featuring live acts and a restaurant. Once inside the elevator I introduced myself. "My name is Xavier, what's yours?"

"Susan," she replied. "Where are you taking me?"

"The jazz club is on the third floor," I answered. "It's quieter and we can talk, unless of course you just wanna stay in the elevator." I winked at her.

She laughed, "No, that's okay, the jazz club is fine."

When the doors opened, I offered my arm and walked her to a booth. I bought her a drink, but she wouldn't have anything stronger than soda. The look on her face when I ordered a Jack Daniels made me wonder. It turned out that I had been wrong about Susan coming from a wedding. She was a tourist from upstate New York visiting relatives in the city. She was wearing her church clothes. I found this somewhat humorous. What was she gonna tell me next, that she was a virgin too? Despite my greatly diminished interest, I went through the motions anyway. When I asked for her phone number, she agreed to give it, but just then a young woman approached our table. Susan introduced me to her cousin and excused herself so they could talk.

While they were gone, Daisy suddenly slid into the booth. "There you are! I've been looking all over for you."

"Why would you be looking for me?" I asked, "I thought you and my sister were competing to see who would get the most phone numbers."

Daisy looked shocked, "Is that what she told you? I can't believe she told you that."

"She didn't tell me anything," I replied, "I just know my sister. But you won't get too many numbers sitting here. Why don't you go back downstairs?"

"You promised me a foot massage." she said as she kicked off her heels and put her feet in my lap.

Susan was coming back towards the booth but when she saw that someone had taken her place, she shook her head, turned and walked away. As she did, I saw her crumpling a piece of paper.

I considered going after her, but instead I looked at Daisy. "What are you doing?"

We both knew she had very carefully timed her entrance to ruin my chances with Susan, but looking as innocent as possible she answered, "I just want the foot massage you promised me."

Daisy looked more desirable than ever. With her feet in my lap, her tiny skirt barely covered her panties and I expected a breast to pop out of her skimpy top at any moment. Seeing the mix of defiance and innocence in her eyes made her look extremely sexy. She might be my sister's best friend, but she was the one provoking me.

I took a foot in my hands and started to rub the sole with my thumbs. Every time I applied even the slightest pressure, Daisy jumped as if startled. With her head cocked back, I had no problem staring at her breasts as they jiggled. I doubt I would have had this much fun with Susan.

Just when we started to really get into it, I saw my sister coming and I gently pushed Daisy's feet off my lap. From my sister's body language, I could tell she was annoyed. I just leaned back and smiled.

"I was looking for you guys," Sis said.

"Why?" I asked.

"It's getting late," she said, "time to go home."

"Gosh," I mocked, looking at my watch, "look at the time."

Daisy frowned, but I ignored her as I slid out of the booth.

The subway ride back to Brooklyn was quiet. Daisy was mad at my sister for interrupting us, my sister was mad at Daisy for making it obvious that she liked me, and both were mad at me for not taking a position one way or another. Interestingly, I actually felt I was the only one with a legitimate reason to be upset. After all, Susan was about to give me her phone number. Still, I wasn't holding any grudges; I just sat there smiling.

The next day, I drove Daisy back to her aunt's house. She gave me her number in Florida, I gave her my numbers in Haïti, and we promised to stay in touch.

Later that night, during the drive back to New Jersey, I tried to have a talk with my sister. "Poupette, I hope you're not mad about Daisy."

"Look," she said angrily, "I don't give a shit what the two of you do. I told her you were a dog, if she's too stupid to listen then forget her."

"Hey wait just one second," I said, genuinely hurt. "What the hell do you mean I'm a dog? And you didn't actually tell her that, did you?"

Sis was defiant. "I mean the way you chase women. You're a dog! And yes, I most certainly did tell her. I warned her before she met you. But does she listen? No, of course not, instead she throws herself at you."

"Look," I protested. "It's not like that at all."

Sis interrupted, "Don't give me that shit! I'm your sister. I know you. You're just gonna hurt her like all the others." My sister was close to tears. "Why couldn't you just leave her alone? Do you have to fuck every girl you see? She's my best friend."

I was stunned. For years, I had tried to portray myself to my sister as a gentleman, but in an instant I realized she had seen through the facade to the real me. "Poupette listen, I'm sorry. I never meant to hurt anyone."

Sis interrupted again, "Don't you understand? Daisy's in love with you!"

I swallowed hard. "She told you that?"

My sister let out a heavy sigh. "Daisy is my best friend, she didn't have to tell me."

Okay, at that point it was clear I had really fucked up bad. "Look Poupette, I'm really sorry but I never touched her. I mean I did, but not like that, I've never even kissed her. I don't know where Daisy is getting this shit from."

"Maybe it's all the times you stayed on the phone 'til three a.m.," Sis said sarcastically. "Or the fact that you promised to fly to Miami to be with her for your birthday."

In a flash of anger, I shouted, "Holy shit man! Do you girls blab about everything?" After taking a deep breath, I added softly, "Look, I'm really sorry that this all got blown out of proportion, but you don't need to worry about me messing with your friend. Like I told you, I don't do virgins."

Sis was shaking her head, "Yeah, I know, you just lead them on…" and she added under her breath "…dog."

I turned up the radio, and not much else was said the rest of the drive back to Mom's house. Two days later, I was on a plane heading back to Port-au-Prince.

Chapter 10
"Home Again"

On the flight back, I thought about my vacation. I had been drunk the entire time. But worse, I had barely given Liz a thought. I hadn't missed her in the slightest bit. Even as I was flying back to her, I wasn't looking forward to it. I tried to remember what it was like making love to her, but all I got were pornographic images completely devoid of any emotion even remotely resembling love. Whatever had existed between us, there was no doubt in my mind that it was completely gone. I should have felt sadness, but what I felt was far worse: a feeling of emptiness so unbearable that it cried out for immediate relief. I signaled the stewardess and ordered another Johnny Walker on ice.

I don't even like Johnny Walker, but after a few drinks I was able to relax and soon drifted into that state of reverie that long flights always seem to induce. My thoughts turned to my boss, Tony. He was a man I greatly admired, not only because he had mentored me, but because he had a lifestyle I found equally admirable. Tony wasn't a rich man, but he owned his own airplane, and at least one weekend a month he would fly to the Dominican Republic in his single-engine Rockwell Challenger to play golf.

Earlier that year Tony, Frank (the general services manager) and I were scheduled to fly to Fort Lauderdale to meet with one of our purchasing agents. Rather than fly commercial, Tony decided it would be more fun to fly up there in his airplane. Frank and I eagerly agreed.

⋙:⋘

Our appointment was for first thing Monday morning, but Tony wanted to leave Friday around noon. According to him, a direct flight would be six hours, but we would be making two stops. First, we were stopping in Puerto Plata (a city in the northern part of the Dominican Republic) for fuel, then were to land in the Bahamas to stretch our legs and get a bite to eat. In any case, it would be well after sunset when we landed at Fort Lauderdale/Hollywood International Airport.

When we got to civil aviation, Tony drove around to the small field where private planes were parked. I'd flown in small airplanes many times as part of my job so I wasn't worried, but the Challenger looked smaller than I expected. We stowed our three small suitcases in the tail of the airplane and entered the cockpit. The plane was designed to seat four adults but I couldn't imagine anyone larger than me sitting in the back. This meant that Frank, being a burly guy, sat up front by necessity. The weather on that January afternoon was perfect for flying and visibility couldn't have been better. We took off without incident and headed northeast.

When we landed in Puerto Plata two hours later, Tony treated us to lunch. He was decidedly more relaxed than usual. For all the indulgence he showed me, Tony applied the strictest standards of professionalism to himself. He was always at his desk five minutes before it was time to start work, and his desk was always immaculate. When Tony asked for an answer he expected a complete, precise answer, in writing, using perfect grammar and as few words as possible to convey the answer. If Tony asked for something to be done, the same exacting standards were to be applied to every aspect of the task. Frank and I smiled at each other as we realized the 'old man' was finally relaxing a little. Tony had no problem drinking a few beers after work, so there was nothing surprising about him drinking now, but when Tony ordered his third beer, Frank and I exchanged worried glances.

It was Frank who finally asked, "Hey boss, shouldn't we get going? We don't want to land too late."

Tony smiled as he finished his beer. "Yeah, you're probably right."

After using the restroom, we gathered our stuff and walked out to the plane. It was now fully fueled, but it was mid-afternoon. Frank and I boarded while Tony took his time inspecting the outside of the plane. When Tony finally got in, he turned the ignition but all he got was a click. He tried again but the engine still wouldn't start. "Well, I'll be damned," Tony said with a raised eyebrow.

"Boss, what's wrong?" Frank asked.

"She won't start," Tony said, stating the obvious.

"So what do we do now?" I asked.

"Well, it's too late to get a mechanic," Tony started, "so the best thing to do is take a taxi into town and come back in the morning."

Frank looked at Tony. "Whatever you say boss," he replied, then turned and looked at me. We were both confused. For a man whose airplane had just broken down, Tony was surprisingly calm. Oh well, if Tony wasn't concerned, then why should we be?

We took a taxi into town, found some inexpensive hotel rooms across the street from the beach, and after putting our bags away we met on the terrace of the hotel for more beers. By that time, Frank and I were starting to suspect that Tony had planned all this. As I gazed out across the ocean, thinking what a beautiful day it was, a gorgeous Dominican girl stopped to look at me from across the street. She appeared to be about eighteen, with wavy black hair cascading off her shoulders and onto her back. She was wearing tight, denim shorts, a bikini top, flip-flops and had a brightly colored backpack slung over her shoulder. Judging from her wet hair and the way she was dressed, it was obvious she was coming from the beach. I looked at Tony. "Boss, what do you think?"

Tony laughed, "Why are you asking me? Get her over here."

I called her over and invited her to join us. Her name was Carolina. She spoke no English but I spoke enough broken Spanish to make myself understood.

After a while Tony got impatient. "Quit wasting time and ask her if she has friends."

Surprised, I said, "Sure boss." Then I turned to Carolina and translated the question.

She smiled at Tony and said, "Si señor, momentito por favor." And with that she got up and walked away. A few minutes later, she came back with two more hot babes.

Man, I thought to myself, this is great! After introductions, we all agreed to meet on the terrace in a couple of hours and go out for dinner and drinks.

That night the six of us went to a nice Italian restaurant. Tony paid for everything. After that we went to a club. The entire time, Carolina was attentive, laughed at all my jokes and seemed absolutely delighted to be in my company. After a few hours of dancing, Carolina and I walked back to my hotel room. Just as I was getting ready to smooth talk her into spending the night with me, she asked, "One hour, two hours, or all night?"

I wasn't sure I heard right so I asked her to repeat. For the first time since I had met her, Carolina looked annoyed. She repeated her question and held her hand out, palm up. Damn! Carolina was a fucking hooker! I felt a surge of anger rising from deep inside as I realized what a fool I had been. I wanted to slap the shit out of her. But I knew she hadn't actually done anything to deserve that. I shook my head in frustration. "Not interested!" I turned to open my door and she tapped me on the shoulder. When I asked what she wanted, she explained that she expected to be compensated for the time she had spent with me. Before I knew it, I was yelling at her in English. "Bitch, get the fuck out my face!" I have no idea if she understood the words or not, but she got the message and left. Of course, after that I really needed a drink, so I went to the nearest bar.

I have no idea how I made it back to the hotel, but the next morning Tony came knocking and we all took a taxi back to the airport. Not surprisingly, when we got to the plane, Tony fixed the "problem" in a few seconds. He had a big grin on his face when he climbed into the cockpit, and we were off the ground and headed for the Bahamas a few minutes later.

❧:☙

I opened my eyes when I realized I was laughing out loud. I couldn't stop thinking of the look on Joey's face the night I met Nicole. I must have had the same look as I faced off with Carolina. Hard to believe that night in Puerto Plata had happened only seven months earlier. I got a couple of strange looks from some other passengers but I ignored them. Instead of using the call button, I looked down the aisle and waved to the nearest stewardess. It was time for another drink.

When the plane landed, I cleared customs, retrieved my bags and waited outside for my driver. After a few minutes, I called the dispatcher on my two-way radio only to be informed no one was scheduled to pick me up, but that someone would be sent as soon as possible. I told the dispatcher to forget it and I called home. When Mary answered the phone, she sounded so happy to hear me that I couldn't help smiling myself. Before I knew it, Nelson was there and we were driving home. Soon after I walked in, Pop and I were having a drink together while Mary got dinner ready.

That evening I felt very restless. I'd been back for hours and I hadn't called Liz yet. Despite feeling guilty about that, another far stronger feeling compelled me. It was a thirst for a particular ambiance, a craving for the bawdy crowd of the Flamenco bar.

After taking a shower, I dressed, took Pop's car, and drove to the Flamenco. Everyone was glad to see me and commented on how much weight I had gained and how good I looked. I was hoping to see Nicole, but she never showed up. There were several girls

I could have left with, but reluctantly I had a few more drinks and went home alone.

The next day I called Liz. She wanted to know why I didn't call as soon as I had gotten home? Why I hadn't called even once while I was away? And, when was she going to see me? I ignored the first two questions and assured her that she would see me later in the day. A few hours and quite a few drinks later, I went to see her. When I arrived, Liz was smiling but she looked sad. For a moment we both hesitated, then I put my arms around her and kissed her. Liz kissed me with passion and I did my best to match her intensity. When we broke apart, she spoke first. "I missed you, Xavier."

"I missed you too," I lied.

"But you never called," she said.

"Baby, I'm sorry," I said, at a loss for words. In an attempt to get some control of the situation I pulled her close so I could caress her back.

Liz pulled away. "No Xavier. Talk to me. What's going on?"

"Sweetheart, I don't know what you're talking about," I said.

"How could you not know?" she asked. "You haven't seen me in three weeks and you have to get drunk before you can come spend some time with me. What am I supposed to think?" Liz waited for an answer but when it was clear that none was forthcoming, she continued. "Does that seem normal to you, Xavier?"

Desperate to gain the upper hand I played the sympathy card. "Honey, I know you're right but I've had a lot on my mind. The doctors all looked at my neck and it looks really bad. Permanent damage."

Liz's tone changed immediately. "Oh my God. Baby, are you going to be okay?"

Relieved the emotional balance had shifted in my favor, I continued the ruse. "Well, there's not much more they can do now, but I may have to fly back up there in a few months."

Liz wrapped her arms around me. "Baby, I'm sorry I gave you a hard time. But I'm your girl. You don't have to go through this alone. I'm here for you."

I started to gently caress her back. "I know you are. I should have called you while I was away, but I didn't want to worry you. Forgive me baby. I was wrong."

Liz squeezed even more tightly. "It's okay, I understand."

I could feel the tension finally leave her shoulders as I continued to caress her back. I leaned forward and whispered in her ear, "I missed you."

That night, I took Liz to the Flamenco for dinner. Though she knew I was a regular, I had never taken her there and she never asked why. We arrived dressed like we were going to a cocktail party. I was wearing navy trousers and a burgundy shirt. Liz wore an asymmetrically cut, midnight blue dress and heels. Her hair was up, revealing her long, slender neck. Pearls hung from two-inch gold chains on each ear. The matching gold chain around her neck had a pearl every two inches. Liz was beautiful. I opened the car door for her, offered my arm and walked her the short distance to the entrance. The security guard stood up as we approached and greeted us with a huge Cheshire cat smile. "Good evening Mr. Xavier, good evening Madame."

I wondered why he was acting like such an idiot, but politely I said, "Evening Max."

Liz just smiled at him as we walked in. Heading down the hall, I got a strange feeling in the pit of my stomach. Maybe it was a big mistake bringing Liz there. But it was already too late. We descended the steps down to the bar, and everyone turned to look at us. The place was full of regulars. I knew just about everyone there. Bryan and Roland both smiled from behind the bar; in fact, all the men were smiling. Many of the women were smiling too, but a few weren't as they sized up Liz. I walked past the bar with what I hoped was a neutral smile, and gave a general wave as I continued walking with Liz.

My intention had been to walk past the bar and straight into the restaurant, but Roland came around the ban with a big grin and cut us off as he extended a hand to Liz. "Welcome to the Flamenco."

Liz shook his hand as I made the introduction. "Liz, this is Roland, one of the owners and one of my best friends. Roland, this is Liz." By then, Liz had put her free hand back on my arm. After an awkward pause, Liz squeezed my arm and I realized she and Roland were both waiting for me to elaborate. "Liz is my girlfriend."

"Oh, that's wonderful," Roland said with an even bigger smile. "No wonder we haven't been seeing you as much lately. Now that I've met Liz, I can see why you wanted to keep her all to yourself. Let me get you guys a waiter."

Liz was all smiles as Roland signaled for a waiter to come forward. Even with our backs to the bar I could feel several dozen sets of eyes boring a hole in the back of my head. By the time we were seated, it had only been a few seconds, but it had felt like an hour. After helping Liz with her chair and putting a menu in front of each of us, our waiter was about to go but I stopped him. "Paul, please bring us a bottle of Concha y Toro."

Before Paul could answer, Liz interrupted, "Honey, we don't need a whole bottle of wine," then she turned to Paul, "Two glasses will be fine."

"Yes Madame," Paul answered.

"Wait!" I said, "I'm gonna want more than one glass."

Liz put a hand on my arm. "Baby, you can have another glass, but you don't need a whole bottle." She looked at me with pleading eyes and said softly so only I could hear, "Please baby, for me."

Turning to Paul, who couldn't help smiling as he stood there waiting for us to finish, I put on a fake smile and said, "Well, there we have it, two glasses of red wine."

Paul nodded. "Right away Mr. Xavier," he said, and then turned and left us.

Liz moved her chair closer to mine and put a hand on my knee. "Baby, please don't be mad, but you don't need to drink so much." As her hand moved up my leg she continued. "You don't need alcohol, you have me. Drink me baby. As much as you want, anytime you want." She leaned forward and kissed me on the ear.

I turned towards her and kissed her. It was a little kiss with very little feeling behind it. "Okay baby, you're right. I'll try to drink less."

Somewhat appeased, Liz said, "Thank you baby."

Not much was said during the meal. Liz tried to get me to talk about my trip, but I insisted there wasn't much to say. Halfway through dinner I excused myself to go to the restroom. When I got to the bar, I ignored everyone, went straight to Bryan and ordered a double shot of Jack Daniels. After swallowing it in one gulp, I turned to find Renaldo, the Mexican diplomat, standing next to me. "Hey Renaldo, how you been?"

Renaldo was a very nice man in his sixties. Tilting his head downward so he could look at me above the edge of his wire-rimmed glasses, he smiled and spoke with his heavy Latin accent. "That's a very lovely lady you have there Xavier. You sure you want to leave her alone? It would be a shame if someone snatched her up." As he said it, Renaldo threw a quick glance towards Bryan.

Renaldo was always watching out for me. Like everyone else, he knew about my break up with Alice, but he was the only one to voice an objection when she had shacked up with Bryan. I felt obliged to smile back, but the last thing I wanted was more advice, or more smiles for that matter. "Don't worry my friend, I'm not leaving her alone for long, but I have to visit the restroom." With that, I turned and headed up the stairs.

I was in a sour mood. All I wanted was to be left alone to drink in peace. As I walked with my head down, my thoughts grew dark. Inside my head a storm was brewing. Angry clouds of wrath gathered above and around me when suddenly... the sun broke through. It was Nicole putting a hand on my shoulder, "Xavier, are you okay?"

My momentum carried me right into her path and I had to wrap my arms around her to keep from knocking her over. "Oh shit! Nicole, I'm sorry, I didn't see you."

"You must be really distracted," she said, "what's going on?"

When I realized she was still in my arms, I reluctantly let her go. "Oh, it's nothing, just a lot on my mind. So how are you?"

Nicole looked up into my eyes. "Okay I guess. I don't see you anymore."

At that moment, I wanted nothing more than to leave with Nicole, but that was impossible. "I've been out of the country... on business. But we should catch up."

"That would be nice," she said. "We never did get to go to the beach."

"Yes, you're right," I said, "I guess I owe you."

"I hope you're not leaving," she said.

Suddenly, I remembered Liz. "No, no I'm not, just going to the restroom." After an awkward pause, I said, "Honey, I'd love to talk to you more tonight but I have someone with me. Call me tomorrow and we'll make plans."

"Oh, okay." Nicole was disappointed but as usual she did her best to hide it. "I understand Xavier. I'll see you soon."

Nicole was about to walk away but I held her hand, leaned forward and kissed her tenderly on the lips. "See you later, hon."

I went into the bathroom and washed my hands. When I walked back downstairs, it was my turn to smile as I walked towards the entrance to the restaurant. I ignored all the ladies but winked at Nicole as I walked past her. The clouds were gone for the moment. As I sat back down at our table, Liz looked at me questioningly. I tried to ignore her but it was no use. "What is it?" I asked.

Liz looked at me incredulously. "Baby, you were gone ten minutes and you come back with a big grin on your face. What happened?"

I eased back in my seat. "Oh, I'm sorry baby. The guys at the bar kept me talking and joking. Anyway, you have me all to yourself now." I leaned forward, kissed her and went back to my meal.

When we were both done, Paul presented me with the check and a pen on a platter. After I signed it, he thanked me, nodded to Liz, then turned and walked away with the tray. On our way out, I was hoping we wouldn't have to stop, but of course Liz insisted we say goodbye to Roland. When we got to the bar I introduced Liz to Bryan, who informed us Roland had gone upstairs and would be back shortly. As luck would have it, we were standing right behind Nicole, who turned when she heard my voice. When Nicole saw Liz holding my arm, a look of envy flashed across her face, but it was gone as quickly as it had appeared. Unsure of what would happen next, I waited until Nicole spoke. "So Xavier, who is your friend?"

I smiled at both girls in turn, "Nicole, this is Liz. Liz, this is Nicole. Would you ladies please excuse me?" And with that, I walked to the end of the bar and sat on a stool. Jacky appeared immediately and placed a beer in front of me and waited.

"A glass of red wine for my date, and get Nicole another of whatever she was drinking," I said.

"That won't be necessary." It was Liz speaking from behind me. "Baby let's go."

I looked at Jacky and shrugged my shoulders. "Oh well, I guess it's just a beer." I stepped away from the bar with the bottle in my right hand. Before I could offer it, Liz took my left arm and guided us towards the stairs. I walked slowly, defiantly, as I drank my beer, then Liz stopped abruptly and said, "You forgot to pay for that."

I started up the stairs. "I didn't forget, I have a running tab."

Liz followed behind me. "But you didn't sign."

I took a long sip of my beer as I continued up the stairs. "I only sign for meals. Drinks are just added to my tab."

Once we were in the hallway, Liz stopped me. "Baby listen, I'm not trying to tell you how to run your life, but this is important. You don't even check the bar tab?"

I let out a heavy sigh. "Bryan checks my tab at the end of the night and signs it for me. At the end of the month he gives me the total and I pay. Can we go now?"

Liz wasn't moving. "How much, Xavier?"

I had no idea what she was talking about, but the storm clouds were gathering again. "How much what?"

Liz just stood there looking at me. "How much do you spend a month, on average?"

"What the fuck difference does it make?" I shouted.

Liz kept her calm. "Don't get mad baby. Just tell me how much and I'll drop it."

I leaned against the wall and finished my beer. "About $600."

Liz' eyes opened wide. "Every month?" She shook her head. "What about the girls? When you walk out with one of them, is that covered in the $600 or is that extra?"

I flashed an angry look at Liz and fixed my eyes on hers. "Where the fuck did that come from?"

Liz held her ground. "I saw how they all looked at you. How many of those girls have you slept with, Xavier?"

I took a slow, deep breath and willed myself to remain calm. Still looking in Liz' eyes I forced a cold, cruel smile. "Are you sure you wanna know?"

Liz lowered her eyes. "No, no I don't."

"Then don't fucking ask," I said angrily.

We could hear footsteps coming up the stairs. Liz took my hand and started pulling. "Let's go. Just take me home."

I was still leaning against the wall as I pulled my hand back. When I turned to see who was coming up the stairs, I saw Nicole. Our eyes crossed for a second, then she ducked into the restroom. In a gruff voice I said, "Yeah, let's get the fuck out of here."

As we walked past Max, I handed him the empty bottle. He said good night and I heard Liz answer him, but I just kept walking to the car.

Inside the car neither of us said a word. When Liz realized I was driving to my house she finally spoke. "Xavier, take me home. I'm not spending the night with you."

Liz had defied my authority several times that night and I had to reestablish the balance of power once and for all. In a calm voice, I said, "I beg to differ. What happened to drink me as much as you want, whenever you want? Besides, it's been three weeks and I'm very thirsty."

"Xavier, I'm serious. I'm not in the mood." The anxiety in her voice was unmistakable.

Ignoring her, I put a hand on her exposed thigh.

Liz tried to push my hand. "Don't touch me."

I swatted her hand away and felt my way between her legs.

Gathering her courage, Liz tried again. "Xavier stop."

But the softness of her thighs was turning me on as I continued groping her. "You know what? I'm willing to bet that you're just as thirsty as I am." Abruptly, I took my hand from between her legs and reached into the top of her dress. As usual, she wore no bra so finding her nipples was easy.

Liz was silent until her nipples started to react to my touch, then she turned away from me so that it was impossible to fondle her and drive at the same time. "Xavier, why are you doing this?"

"Isn't it obvious?" I said. "I can pull over and take what's mine right here in the car, but wouldn't you rather do it on a bed? One way or another I'm having you."

I started to caress her back. She resisted at first but after a bit, she sat upright in her seat. This time when I put my hand between her legs she spread to accommodate me and I could feel the moistness through her panties. As I teased her outer lips through the thin fabric, Liz closed her eyes and reclined her seat back. When I moved to her clit, she kicked off her right sandal and put her foot on the dashboard. She gripped the door handle with her right hand, grabbed my wrist with her left hand and encouraged me to go harder. Before long, I was fingering her and smiling to myself.

When we got to my house, I let us in quickly and we immediately started taking our clothes off. There was no lovemaking, just fucking. Like two animals in heat, we fucked through the night. One moment, she was my bitch, the next moment I was her john. Three weeks of pent up frustration drove us both crazy with lust as I pushed myself to give her everything I had and she, with every thrust of my hips, begged for more. In a moment of madness, I felt the connection we once had. It was real and it was strong. It was her screaming my name as I whispered the three magic words into her ear. It was us becoming one as stars exploded around us in one simultaneous orgasm after another. It was needing each other like we were the last two people on earth. It was all those things and more, but it wasn't love. It had never been love. Three months earlier, I would have done anything for this woman. Now, she was just a great fuck. She was still the same beautiful, intelligent, loveable girl I had fallen for. Consequently, I had to conclude that I was incapable of feeling love. I was resigned to that sad reality and consoled myself with the fact that, until further notice and no matter what, Liz was still my property, and there was something strangely comforting in that.

Chapter 11
"Spiraling Down"

The trip to New Jersey had changed me. I had no idea what happened or how it happened, but I was different. Something inside me had broken during those three weeks of binge drinking. My drinking had been bad for a while, but it had become totally out of control. Not only was I drinking every day, but I actually needed to drink in order to function. But that was only the beginning of the insanity.

As my condition got worse, Liz and I had less and less to talk about. Our relationship became a matter of sexual convenience, without even the pretense of romance. When it came to sex, Liz always had my full attention, so there were no complaints in that department, and she accorded me the same courtesy. It was all I could offer her and it was an arrangement she learned to live with.

I called Daisy several times and even entertained the idea of actually visiting her in Miami. She really wanted me to spend my birthday with her so she could make it special, but after careful consideration, I decided to do Daisy a big favor and not call her anymore. I would only bring her grief and misery, and I had way too much on my plate to allow myself to be the object of yet another schoolgirl's crush. Instead of calling to tell her I wasn't coming, I just stopped calling. My birthday was months away and I was sure she would get the hint.

I never did take Nicole to the beach. Since my primary interest was sex, it made no sense to drive all the way to the beach just to fuck her when I had a perfectly good bed at home. So, she was a guest in my bed on many occasions until she moved to another part of town and we lost touch for a while.

The real problem was my job at The Agency. My ability to work became severely impaired. Thanks to my staff, the problem stayed hidden through the end of summer and well into fall, but when I started blacking out at work there was little they could do. Matters got much worse when Tony was reassigned to another country office. With Tony, I got away with murder. No request coming from me was ever considered excessive. I didn't even have a budget. I simply requisitioned what I wanted and Tony signed off on it. In just about everything else like attendance, use of Agency property, overtime for my driver and expense accounts, I also had freedom to do pretty much as I pleased. With the arrival of a new director, I was suddenly under intense scrutiny and most of my perks vanished overnight.

When I woke up one day in my office and had no idea how I had gotten there, that was the beginning of the end. It was early afternoon, I was sitting in my office and I couldn't account for the previous eighteen hours. Since I was wearing the same clothes I had been wearing the day before, it was safe to assume that I had never gone home. I was at a complete loss and I had no idea what to do. I just stared at the clock in disbelief. Eventually, the new director came to my office to check in on me. He didn't say anything; he just made quick eye contact and left.

My mind started racing as I tried to imagine what must have been going through his head. There was no word to describe what I felt. It was a cocktail of shame, guilt, and dread, mixed with uncertainty and served with a large dose of self-loathing.

My head was throbbing, my joints ached, my mouth was pasty and tasted of rotting flesh. I tried to get up, but my knees buckled and I fell back into my chair. Even as the room spun around me, I knew there was only one solution. I was in desperate need of relief so I prayed: "Dear God, if I have ever needed You, it's now. I know I've been unfaithful and I don't deserve Your help. So many times before, You bailed me out and I never kept my promises to You. You've even gotten me out of messes when I was too ashamed to pray. So please Lord, I'm begging You now. If I could have just one drink… maybe two; just enough to clear my mind and help me think straight, I would be ever so grateful." Despite the sincerity of my urgent appeal, the only answer was the pounding in my head. God had abandoned me and alcohol, my truest friend, was nowhere to be found. I was utterly alone with no more than this nameless feeling to keep me company.

I forced myself to think logically. I desperately needed a drink and sitting there wasn't helping me. I had to find a way out of that mess. The building was full of people and I had to stay away from all of them. It was one-thirty in the afternoon. Hopefully, no one would come in my office for the next two hours, and then the building would start clearing out for the day. I would wait an extra thirty minutes to make sure I didn't run into anyone, then I would make my exit.

My all-consuming need for alcohol made the passage of time agonizingly slow as I waited for everyone to go home. Only the shame of being seen in my current condition kept me from leaving any sooner. Eventually, I felt it was safe and I left my office. First, I went to the nearest water cooler and drank my fill, then I ducked into the men's room to relieve myself. With these basics out of the way, I was ready to leave the building. I took a deep breath before leaving the safety of the bathroom and made my way quickly down the stairs and out the front entrance. After walking across the parking lot, I waited nervously for the security guard to let me out of the gate.

When he realized it was me, he looked surprised. "Mr. Xavier, aren't you gonna wait for your driver?"

"No, not today," I answered, "but I'm not going far." Once the gate was opened, I hurried out and started down the street.

Up until then, I had been very weak, but knowing that a stiff drink was only a few blocks away gave me renewed energy and added a spring to my step. When I got to the Flamenco, it was closed and both Bryan and Roland were out running errands, but Max let me in and locked the gate behind me. Once I was downstairs, I decided against hard liquor and pulled a beer out of the large cooler behind the bar. After taking a long, satisfying swig, I felt immediate relief. I found a receipt pad, wrote my name at the top and put two Coronas and a pack of Marlboros on the bill. After a few more swigs, I put the empty bottle on the bar and pulled another one out of the cooler. Less than five minutes after I had walked into the place, there were two empties on the bar.

I grabbed a pack of cigarettes from the display on the windowsill, opened it, pulled one out, broke off the filter and lit up. I inhaled deeply, then sighed in relief, but decided that after all I'd been through a special treat was in order. I scanned the bottles on the shelves and looked for the one with the long blade of buffalo grass in it. I hated vodka, but Zubrowka wasn't just an exception, it was my second favorite spirit after Jack Daniels. Something about the fragrant bison grass made it exceptionally smooth. After finding my treasure I filled a shot glass, but rather than belt it down as I normally would have done, I savored every precious drop. Even as I took my time with my shot of vodka, I could feel the relaxing effect of the two beers and the nicotine. The pain I had felt between my shoulder blades was gone and I sat upright on the stool. My headache was easing off and the beers had washed the nasty taste out of my mouth. I felt much better, but when I looked in the mirror, I realized that I still looked like shit; my lips were badly chapped, my face was greasy and my hair was uncombed. In addition, my clothes were rumpled and dirty, and I was in desperate need of a shower.

It was time to get the hell out of there. I didn't want to be seen at the Flamenco looking as bad as I did, so I called Nelson and instructed him to pick me up at the bus stop. After adding the vodka to my tab and signing the bottom, I finished my drink and went upstairs to the bathroom. Splashing my face with cool water brought almost as much relief as the drinks. I'd be back later that night to get some answers but right then I needed to get home to eat and rest. After

Max let me out, I made my way quickly to the bus stop near the Pétion-Ville market.

I didn't have to wait long for Nelson to get there. Before he could say much, I made it clear that I wasn't in a mood to talk or answer any nosy questions. I just wanted to be driven home as quickly as possible. When I entered the house, Mary was given the same warning. I requested food be brought to my room and I took a beer with me into the shower. After my shower I had no appetite, but I knew it was important that I eat so I got high. Within thirty minutes, my stomach was full and I was dreaming strange dreams.

I awoke late that night feeling a little sore but well-rested. Convinced that I was waking up from a bad dream about losing a day in my life, I sat up in bed and retraced my steps backwards in time. I remembered coming home and taking a shower. I remembered my shot of Zubrowka. I remembered walking from the office to the Flamenco. I remembered waking up in my office. I even remembered the look on the director's face, but that was the end of the line. Beyond that, there were no memories.

I dressed quickly and made my way quietly upstairs. Everyone was asleep. Without turning on the lights, I found Pop's keys where he usually left them, and went back downstairs. Making as little noise as possible, I let myself into the lower courtyard and out to the front gate. Opening and closing the gate by myself, without making noise, was a serious pain in the ass, but I didn't want anyone to know I was out.

When I got to the Flamenco there were only a few people at the bar. From talking to Roland, I found out that he and I had closed the Flamenco together the night before. Bryan had gone to sleep but Roland and I had walked to a strip club that had recently opened several blocks away. Apparently, they were about to close and refused to serve us. Roland and I made lots of noise until they finally agreed to sell us a couple of beers. After that, Roland and I returned to the Flamenco for one last drink, on him, after which he went to bed and I left.

So far so good. The only gap left to fill was between four a.m. and when I woke up in the office. After talking to Roland, I finished my drink and went outside. I was getting ready to drive back home when I saw a group of street kids coming towards me. John and Timmy were among them. I walked towards my car and leaned against the door as they gathered around me.

"Mr. Xavier, are you okay?" John asked.

"I'm okay," I answered. Looking them over, I could tell they knew something. "What happened last night boys?"

I listened carefully as the boys filled me in on the events of the previous night. They confirmed that I had gone to the strip club with Roland but that we didn't stay long. In fact, Roland and I threatened to tear the place apart if they didn't let us in, but the most they would do was sell us a couple of beers and we walked back to the Flamenco. A half hour later, I walked out alone and staggered down the street. John and his friends saw me and tried to talk to me but they couldn't understand a word I was saying. I could barely stand up, much less walk. They helped me back to the Flamenco, but I insisted on sitting on the sidewalk across from the restaurant. I told them all I needed was a bit of rest. Once I sat down, I was unconscious within seconds. John and his friends sat around me and kept guard until sunrise. Finally, with the light and heat of day, I awoke very disoriented. The boys tried to convince me to go home but I insisted on going to work. They walked the four blocks with me until they were within a hundred feet of the gate. They didn't dare get any closer, but they waited until they saw me go inside the gate before leaving. According to them it was about seven a.m.

I thanked the boys, reached into my wallet, pulled out a $20 bill and handed it to John. "Here, you boys get yourselves something to eat. I gotta go." I would have sat in the car to process what I had just heard but the boys wouldn't leave until they saw the car pull away. I drove down the street and made a left at the corner, heading towards the market. My head was swirling as I tried to wrap my brain around the thought I had slept on the sidewalk like a common bum. Driving past one of the side streets leading away from the market, I caught a glimpse of shadowy silhouettes gathered around maggot-infested heaps of trash. With a bit of luck their next meal would be tossed on top of the piles when the vegetable vendors set up their stands at the rising of the sun. For the first time, I realized that the only thing separating me from the poorest beggar was the mere abstraction of perceived wealth. I drove home slowly, my spirit crushed; I was totally demoralized. For once I didn't want to drink, I just wanted to die.

The next day, I went to work under a heavy cloud of shame. As hard as I tried to shake it, the nameless feeling I had birthed the previous day clung to me like a neglected infant screaming for attention. Unable to hold my head up, I hobbled into work hoping to avoid the eyes of my co-workers. This turned out to be the least of my problems, as everyone made a noticeable effort to avoid me.

Later in the day, Jack, the new director, called me to his office. It was the moment I had dreaded, but I also knew it was inevitable. I approached his spacious office and stood in the doorway waiting for instructions.

Jack looked up and invited me to close the door and sit in one of the two chairs facing his large desk. The uncomfortable silence was only broken when he finally closed the thick file folder in front of him and cleared his throat. "So, how are you?"

I didn't think I had any air in my chest but I heard myself mumble the words. "I've been better sir, but I'll be fine."

Jack adjusted his glasses. "Xavier, do you know why I called you into my office?"

Damn, he wouldn't even give me the dignity of a bullet to the head. He wanted me to slit my own wrists right there in front of him. "I suppose, sir, that this has to do with yesterday."

"I guess you can say that," he replied pensively.

The bastard! Instead of just finishing me off, the fucking bastard wanted to play with me. I had been ready to hand him my head on a platter, but fuck that! I decided I wasn't going down without a fight and grabbed the bull by the horns. "Sir, I want to apologize for what happened. I've been neglecting some medical issues for far too long and it all caught up with me yesterday. But I want to reassure you I called my doctor and everything is under control. I'm not gonna sit here and tell you everything is fine, but I will tell you I intend to stop ignoring the problem and do exactly what my doctor tells me. He assures me that with the proper care I'll be fine. In any case, I want you to know that my work won't be affected by this."

Jack leaned back in his chair. "Well, Xavier, I'm glad to hear that. You gave us quite a scare yesterday. Not to mention the effect it had on the rest of the staff."

I jumped in with, "Sir, I can't begin to tell you how embarrassed I am about the whole thing, but it definitely will never happen again."

Jack leaned forward and looked up from his desk. "Xavier, as the new director I have a difficult job. I have to make decisions about people that I've never worked with and all I have to go by are my personal observations and impressions," Jack paused a bit to let that sink in, then glanced at the closed folder in front of him. "And the personnel file."

Okay, if he wanted a fight, I'd give him a fight. When it came to office politics, I was one of the best. I owned that fucking building and everyone in it. He was just an outsider. If anyone in that office had any power at all, I made sure they owed me favors. He might be the director, but he would make the same mistake others had made:

he would underestimate me. I forced myself to remain calm and prepared to counter whatever he was gonna throw at me next.

Jack leaned back in his chair and started again slowly, "Xavier, I'm going to be very honest with you. I had decided to terminate you. The paperwork was done and signed." He looked at me as if testing me but I didn't flinch. He had no choice but to continue. "But when I spoke to Florence, the human resources coordinator, she advised against it. I even spoke to the project managers and they all said the same thing. In reviewing your file, I can see why everyone thinks so highly of you. The fact is, you've been an incredible asset to The Agency." Jack looked at me but I made my face as inscrutable as possible. He continued, "After carefully reviewing all the information available to me, I agree that termination isn't in the best interest of The Agency." Jack tried to break me again with another pause but I held my ground, forcing him to attack. "But there will have to be some changes."

I went on the offensive. "Sir, I completely understand the position you are in and I want to assure you that I also understand the importance of my relationship vis-à-vis The Agency. I won't allow my health problems or anything else to compromise that relationship or in any way diminish the productivity of my department."

Jack's demeanor was as calm and professional as my own. He was no lightweight. "I'm glad to hear that, Xavier. I certainly appreciate that kind of attitude, and it makes me feel even more comfortable with the decision I've made."

Well, I had dodged a bullet and it hadn't even been as hard as I thought it would be. "Thank you sir, you won't regret this." I leaned forward and prepared to stand up and give Jack a firm handshake as I looked him in the eye.

But Jack was still leaning back in his chair. "Xavier, I appreciate your enthusiasm but we recognize that realistically, you can't continue to work like this. You'll need time to take care of yourself.

Finish out this month and make all necessary arrangements with your staff. Effective next month you're going on a three month sabbatical."

I was dumbfounded. "Sabbatical, sir?"

"Yes," Jack started, "of course you'll get half pay while you're out."

He had stunned me but I was fighting for my life and there was no way I would stay down. After regaining my composure, I said, "Sir, I truly appreciate your concern, but with all due respect, I think three months is disproportionate to the severity of the problem. On the other hand, you have a point about me needing time off. I recently used up most of my vacation days but I'm sure I can work something out with Florence." I could feel myself getting hot.

Jack was as cool as a cucumber. "Xavier, you need help, serious help. Alcoholism is a serious disease."

I couldn't believe my ears. Did this son-of-a-bitch just call me an alcoholic? Did he have any fucking idea who he was talking to? Never mind, I would deal with that comment later, but for the time being I had to stay focused on my immediate objective. I forced a smile. "Sir, I can't tell you enough how much I really appreciate the concern and I would be the last person to minimize the issues I'm dealing with, but I have to insist, three months is excessive. A week or two under the care of my doctor, and I'm sure this will all be behind us."

Jack stood up abruptly. "I'm sorry Xavier, but my decision is final. There are no other options on the table." Jack waited for me to stand. I rose slowly to my feet but I couldn't believe this was happening. Once I was standing, Jack came around the desk and put his hands on my shoulders. "Xavier, you're an incredibly bright young man. Don't throw your future away. Get help."

I was speechless. Jack led me to his door, opened it and gave me a firm handshake. "Good luck, Xavier."

After an awkward pause, I managed two words, "Yes sir," turned and walked away. I was too stunned to be angry. All I knew was I had to get the hell out of there. I went to my office and sent an e-mail to my staff advising them I was taking the rest of the day off. My motorcycle had been stolen a week earlier and it was taking a while to get a new one issued to me, so I called Jean and requested a driver to take me home. I explained that it was urgent and I didn't care about the new director's updated policies and procedures. I needed a driver and I needed one immediately. Half an hour later, Jean called to tell me a driver was waiting for me in the parking lot. I shook my head, "the fucking parking lot?" I wanted to give Jean a piece of my mind but I understood that he didn't want to get in trouble. The parking lot wasn't visible from Jack's office. Once we were on our way, I was tempted to stop for a drink but I decided against it and went straight home.

That night, I went to the Flamenco determined to drink as much as I wanted and be at work on time the next day. I didn't have a fucking drinking problem! I just had to be more careful and not drink on an empty stomach. Better nutrition, more rest, exercise, not push myself so hard at work; if I did all those things I'd be fine. Of course having a fucking girlfriend who understood me would be nice too. But fuck Liz. Fuck all the bitches! I didn't need them.

As I sat brooding over a tumbler of Jack Daniels, Bryan came over and sat across from me. "You okay Xavier?"

I looked at Bryan. He'd been my friend for many years. If there was anyone I could talk to, it was him. "Let me ask you something Bryan. Do you think I'm an alcoholic?"

Bryan smiled. "No Xavier, I don't think you're an alcoholic..." Bryan's smile became a grin as he continued, "...you're just a good old-fashioned drunk!" And with that he burst into raucous laughter. It took Bryan a while to realize I wasn't laughing. Once he did, he put a hand on my shoulder and said, "Don't worry buddy, I'm just an old-fashioned drunk myself, so that makes two of us."

I forced a smile, but there was nothing funny about Bryan's comment. He had described me perfectly; alcoholic was too fancy a label for me. I really was just an old-fashioned drunk, exactly the type of person who would sleep on the sidewalk. Bryan offered me a zombie on the house to cheer me up. I gladly accepted it but after just a few more drinks I went home. I needed booze more than ever, but I just couldn't enjoy it like I used to.

There were two weeks left in the month. During that time, Jack expected me to prepare my staff to be completely autonomous. Essentially, he had handed me a shovel and ordered me to dig my own grave. Well, Jack could just fuck himself as far as I was concerned. The only problem was my staff had been running on auto-pilot for months. They were extremely competent, professional and I had trained them well. But more than that, they were so fiercely loyal to me that without my asking, they had already been covering for me. There was nothing left for me to do except write memos and sign the occasional form. When I finally got the nerve to tell them what had been decided, the atmosphere in my office was very somber. Olivia was trying to hide her tears but it was hopeless.

It was Leonard who finally spoke. "Don't worry boss. You'll be back and we'll be here waiting for you."

It was too much to take, so with tears in my eyes and a cracking voice, I asked them to leave before I broke down.

Less than a week from the start of my forced sabbatical, Jean called to tell me a new shipment of motorcycles had come in and one had been reserved for me. I even got a memo from Jack stating that in order to ease the transition I was being allowed to keep both the motorcycle and my notebook computer during the first week of my sabbatical. I was happy to have a bike, but Jack's gesture did nothing to alleviate the bitterness I felt toward him and the entire

Agency. If I had a fucking drinking problem, it was their fucking fault! I had worked myself to the point of burnout in order to bring these bastards into the 20th century. And this was how they reward-ed me.

On my first day out of work, I left the house late in the morning and rode up to Kenscoff, a medium-sized town high up in the moun-tains. Even in summer, the temperature up there rarely made it into the low 80s. But this time of year it might be in the mid-60s if there were no clouds to block the sun. I took my time riding up the moun-tain. Rather than a rush, it was peace that my soul longed for. Riding through the sleepy little town, I remembered the weekends I had spent up there drinking and partying with the Winchesters. Fred and Denise were like adoptive parents. Their son and daughter, Laird and Heather, were like a brother and sister. They had all moved to California years ago and were doing well, except for Laird who had died in an unfortunate accident.

As I stood in front of the house they had lived in, I felt a deep desire to talk to Fred. He would know what to do. If anyone could get me out of this mess, it was Fred. And I would give anything for one of Denise's hugs. Tears were streaming down my cheeks, and before I knew it I had opened the gate and was slowly climbing the sixty-nine steps that led all the way up to the house. To my left was the massive foundation dug into the side of the mountain, and to my right was a maze of hedges and low rock walls. My mind filled with happy memories of playing a drunken version of hide-and-seek in the maze as rock music blared from the house above. Since our games were always played at night, who knew how many kisses were given and stolen among those hedges.

Before I knew it, I was at the huge terrace adjacent to the house. To my surprise there were a dozen tables, each with four chairs. The front door opened and an elegant lady came out and welcomed me. Suddenly I realized how stupid I had been. What had possessed me to just come on private property like this? I wiped the tears from my face as I began to apologize but the lady explained that the house had been turned into a restaurant. However, it was only open on Sundays. Nonetheless, I was welcome to roam around the yard. I thanked her and she went back inside.

As I stood there breathing fresh mountain air and reminiscing on the past, I thought about my life. It had been a fun ride. I had achieved a lot and met many interesting people. Why should I have any regrets? Maybe it was all part of Divine Order. A signal that my time was near. If Destiny was calling, then who was I to resist?

"Xavier... Xavier!"

I heard my name being called, but it was like a dream. At first, it seemed kind of odd that Destiny would have a woman's voice, but the more I thought about it, the more sense it made.

"Xavier, over here!"

Still in a daze, I turned towards the voice. On the front porch of the neighboring house I could see a tall woman with short brown hair, a denim shirt, jeans and cowboy boots. I didn't mind that Destiny was a woman, but the whole western look was kind of a turn-off.

The woman was signaling for me to come join her on her porch. Only then did I realize how lost I had been in my thoughts. I had no idea who this woman was, but she was cute and she obviously knew me. I looked at the wide vegetable garden separating me from her house, and after jumping the fence, I delicately found my way across. I hadn't even noticed that she was holding a beer bottle by her side until she raised it to her mouth and took a swig. When I got to the porch, I stared at the woman's face. She looked about thirty, tall and slim, with well-defined cheekbones, pretty blue eyes and a light dusting of freckles across the bridge of her nose. From the dark circles under her eyes I knew that she either hadn't slept in a while or she had done lots of crying; nonetheless, she was an attractive woman. I had seen her before, but I couldn't remember where or when. Sensing I didn't recognize her, the woman extended her hand. "Remember me, Terry?" Even as I took her hand and smiled, she could tell that the name left me blank. "I'm Fabrice's girlfriend."

I held her hand as I rolled the name in my head. "Fabrice?" Then it hit me. "Omigod, Terry, I'm so embarrassed. Of course it's you."

Satisfied that I recognized her, Terry pulled me into her arms and hugged me. "Geez, what does a girl have to do to get a little love around here?"

"I'm sorry Terry, but this is the first time I've seen you sober."

Terry smiled and spoke with a strong Midwestern accent, "Oh, don't worry, honey, I been drinkin' all day, a couple more beers and I'll be drunk as a skunk."

I laughed. "Actually, I meant it's the first time I'm sober and seeing you."

Once Terry understood the joke, she let out a hearty laugh. It wasn't the laugh of a lady. It was the contagious laugh of an honest country girl. As soon as we could stop laughing long enough to speak, Terry led me into the house. "Well sweetie, we can take care of you too, come on in and have a drink."

I had met Terry less than a week before when she came into the Flamenco with Fabrice Reynolds, heir to one of the richest families in Haïti and an occasional patron of the Flamenco. I'd seen Terry two nights in a row, but I had no memory of the first night. When I walked into the Flamenco the second night, Bryan was very upset and told me I had made a total fool of myself and insulted Fabrice's girlfriend the night before. Bryan insisted I apologize, which I was quite willing to do, but when I tried to apologize to Terry, she had no idea who I was. I explained what Bryan had told me but she admitted she had been so drunk herself that she didn't remember a thing either. We both had a great laugh about it and spent the rest of the night drinking together.

Terry led me into the living room of the well-appointed chalet. A large, semi-circular couch was sunken into the floor and built around a large fireplace, creating the odd effect of a huge nest in the middle of the room. Animal furs were scattered about the floor and trophies were mounted on the wall around the fireplace. After I descended into the nest, Terry brought me a beer and sat next to me. We talked, drank and laughed for hours. Apparently, Fabrice had just broken up with Terry and she was drowning her sorrows. I explained my situation at The Agency and she sympathized. We were a match made in drinker's heaven; instant friends.

Late into the evening, and after many drinks, I finally started on the ninety-minute ride down the mountain. I would ride back up the mountain several times that week and spend the day drinking with Terry. I only stopped going up to Kenscoff when I had to return the bike to The Agency. But I didn't care; I was determined to prove to the world that I didn't have a drinking problem. Of course, the way I chose was to drink more than everybody else and do my best to not black out or make a fool of myself.

A month into my sabbatical, I started thinking that I could really get used to this. Since I didn't have to go to work, I could stay out even later, sleep in all day, and still get paid for it. I spent more and more time with Terry. Funny thing was, she and I never got sexually involved. She was a friend and a drinking partner. We met at the Flamenco occasionally but after the breakup with Fabrice, she decided to open her own bar/restaurant. Fabrice was very generous: he arranged for Terry to take over the lease of the Panda Club, a prime location in Pétion-Ville. Terry renamed the club and called it, of course, Terry's. She renovated the bar and made it a nice hang out. The place was huge. It had a dance club on the second floor and an outdoor area that could host several hundred guests. There was even an outdoor stage. Fabrice insisted that as his ex-girlfriend, Terry was to maintain a high social profile. He even helped promote the new restaurant. Of course, I became a regular, usually starting my night at the Flamenco and ending it at Torry's. I felt free to drink without limit, and I even got used to the increasingly frequent blackouts.

Liz had become a mere afterthought. It was common to go a week or more without even so much as a telephone conversation. But my appetite for sex was boundless. Every night I entertained myself with a different girl. More often than not it was a prostitute who would give me what I wanted, then disappear into the night, but occasionally I would pick up a girl at the Flamenco or one of the other bars. Some nights, one girl just wasn't enough so I would take two. Usually I just drove to some place quiet and had sex in the car, but sometimes, if I was extra horny and wanted to go several rounds, I would take them to a hotel. A few times, I woke up at home, in my own bed, shocked to find a nameless streetwalker cuddled up to me in bed. At first, it was just embarrassing, but when small items started disappearing from the house, I realized how dangerous my habits were becoming. Even so, I was powerless to stop.

It was a month into my sabbatical and I was ten days away from my birthday. I was entering a time of year that I hated. From my birthday on November 10th all the way through Christmas, I maintained the sourest of moods. This had been my habit going back many years. I hated my birthday and I hated the holiday season. Only New Year's Eve, with its round-the-clock drinking, could break the spell as I started each New Year. Yet, the total lack of inhibitions I was experiencing allowed me to think that this year might be different.

Chapter 12
"A Night in the Desert"

Gary Delatour was my kind of guy: a confident, well-spoken man who could handle his liquor and had an eye for the ladies. As a childhood friend of Pop's, it was only natural we would open our house to him when he flew in from New York and needed a place to stay. Apparently, Gary was in some trouble and needed to lay low for a while. Pop assumed Gary would be with us a week or two, but it had already been more than a month and there was no sign he was going anywhere anytime soon.

Since I was on sabbatical, Gary's presence in the house worked out well for me. When it came to night life, he and I complement-ed each other very well. I liked hanging out with him because he seemed to know even more women than I did, and everywhere he took us, women invariably joined. He enjoyed the places I took him because we were always treated like VIPs and of course, I paid for everything. We soon developed a loose pattern: some nights we went to his hangouts, some nights mine, other nights we each went solo. Since we both liked loose women, it was good having someone I could share my lifestyle with. In a strange way, Gary also held me in check. He was twenty-five years my senior, so I deferred to him in many things. Because he suffered from stomach ulcers, we often had to slow our roll and go home earlier than I would have preferred, but I never minded because I enjoyed his company so much.

Mary started complaining that with another man in the house, she was doing a lot more work. Rather than argue, Pop hired a boy to help around the house. Anything to keep Mary happy. The kid was sixteen but he didn't look like he could do any real work. In fact, he was a real pretty-boy. His skin was fair, his facial features were very delicate, and his frame was like that of a preadolescent girl. He looked more like an underage male prostitute than a houseboy, but as if that weren't bad enough, he seemed to feel he was too good for housework. I despised him from the beginning.

A few nights before my birthday, I decided to go out alone. I was sitting at the bar when Fritz entered the Flamenco. Fritz, like most of my close friends, was a retired warrior. He had been an elite under-cover operative of the West German Secret Service before the fall of the Berlin Wall. More recently, he had been in charge of security at the German embassy. Fritz was a good friend but I could go months without seeing him. When he saw me, Fritz gave me a big bear hug; apparently he had come looking specifically for me. Fritz's birthday was Saturday the 11th, the day after mine, and he was opening his new restaurant that night. It would be a triple celebration: two birthdays and a grand opening. When he made it clear I would be the guest of honor, I couldn't refuse.

I bought Fritz a drink, but he didn't stay long. Soon after, I decided to go home. It had been an enjoyable night and I was feeling very good. So good, in fact, that for once I decided to quit while I was ahead. I drove at a leisurely pace while listening to old-school hits on Radio Metropole. I was thoroughly drunk, but I was conscious and functioning normally. To me, this constituted solid evidence that I didn't have a drinking problem and I was very pleased.

I got to the house and I was annoyed but not surprised when I honked and no one came to open the gate. The new houseboy couldn't even do that. Rather than spend ten minutes sitting in the car honking my horn, as I had done several times since he started, I got out and opened the gate. Amazingly, the little fucker had suc-cessfully trained me to open the gate by myself when I got home! I was shaking my head in disbelief as I drove through the open gate, and thought sarcastically, who knows, maybe if I'm good he'll give me Sunday off.

As soon as I saw the house, I knew something was wrong be-cause every light was on. I pulled the Mazda into its designated space. Gary's Mitsubishi Lancer was parked in its usual place. Everything was quiet. I made my way around the side, through the lower courtyard, and to the back door. "What's going on?" I asked, standing in the doorway.

Nelson answered, "In here Mr. Pouchon. We're in Pop's room."

My heart sank. I sprang across the sitting area, past the bathroom and down the hall expecting the worst. Pop's door was open. I rushed in convinced something terrible had happened to him, but nothing could have prepared me for what I saw. Pop was sitting up in bed, clearly intoxicated, and looking very dazed. When he saw me, he smiled drunkenly. Nelson and Gary were both standing at the foot of the bed, and on the floor between them was our new houseboy with his hands and feet tied together behind his back. Next to him was a large butcher knife. When he saw me, the boy tried to speak through his gag, but Nelson silenced him with a solid kick to the ribs.

"What the fuck is going on here?" I yelled.

Nelson looked at the boy as if daring him to make another sound. "It's okay Mr. Pouchon. This boy won't be troubling us anymore. But it was close. If we had walked in just a minute later he would have slit Pop's throat."

Unable to believe what I was hearing, I looked at Pop. He was still smiling at me, but a line of drool was running down the side of his mouth. I turned to Gary. "Gary, help me out here, man, this doesn't make any fucking sense."

Gary took a deep breath before speaking in a calm voice. "What do you want me to tell you? Pop fired the kid this afternoon and told him to get the fuck out of here. The kid sneaks back in tonight, tries to rob us and from the looks of it, he would have made a clean getaway but he decided to kill Pop before leaving with his loot. I just happened to come home at the right time and heard noise, so I called Nelson and we came in here together. He was hiding in the closet."

The boy started to shake his head in protest and tried to mumble, but Nelson gave him another kick to the ribs.

"Nelson!" I couldn't believe this was happening. "Ease off there man, he's not going anywhere!"

It was obvious that Nelson wanted to kick him again for good measure. "Don't feel sorry for him Mr. Pouchon. He's just a fucking thief and a murderer."

I looked at Pop. "What do you have to say in all this?"

Pop shrugged his shoulders and slurred, "What the hell do I know?"

I looked at Gary. "Okay, let's call the police and let them deal with this fucking kid."

"What, are you kiddin' me?" Gary looked down at the boy. "We call the police and all they're gonna do is rough him up, hold him a few days, then let him loose."

Nelson interjected, "I say we finish him off."

I couldn't believe I was hearing this. I turned to Nelson. "What the fuck do you mean, finish him off?"

Nelson was adamant. "Mr. Pouchon, he tried to kill Pop. I say we slit his throat the same as he was gonna do to Pop." At those words, the boy started crying. Nelson gave him another solid kick to the ribs but the tears wouldn't stop.

"Nelson, stop!" I yelled. "We can't just kill him." I looked at Gary and asked, "Can we?"

Gary sighed. "Nelson is right. This kid was gonna kill Pop. If we kill him, we'd be doing the cops a favor, and keeping the streets a bit safer. Who knows how many people this fucking kid has killed and robbed in the middle of the night?"

Right about then, I should have stopped listening to them. I should have insisted that we call the police and let them handle it but I looked at Pop. He was out like a light and snoring softly. Why would anyone want to kill this man? How could anyone even think to do that? I looked at the boy. He made eye contact with me and I could see the pleading look in his eyes. I had seen that look before. I looked more carefully, but in my drunken state, my eyes had trouble focusing. I wouldn't give up until I could see his eyes clearly. He just looked back at me, his eyes pleading for mercy: he was begging for his life. Tears were streaming down his face, but with Nelson standing over him he didn't dare make a sound. He just continued to stare back at me. I looked at the pretty eyes, the long lashes, then the rest of his face, the high cheekbones, the delicate nose, the gently rounded chin until the face I saw was Natasha's. In that instant, I made my decision and turned to Gary. "Okay, how do we do this?"

Gary answered without hesitation, "I agree with Nelson, slit his throat."

I turned to Nelson. "Okay, we slit his throat." Then I asked Gary, "Who's gonna do it?"

Gary spoke calmly and deliberately. "Pop is your father, in his absence you are the man of the house." Gary pointed to Pop. "It is both your duty and your honor to defend him." He looked down at the boy. "Especially from scum like this."

I thought about what Gary had said and it made a lot of sense. Pop was my responsibility. I had to be the man of the house. "Okay, I'll do it."

"Mr. Pouchon, let me soften him up a bit first." Nelson got ready to kick him again.

I stepped between Nelson and the boy. "That's not necessary. Let's just get this over with." I looked at Gary again. "How do I do this?"

Gary stepped forward. "Just take him in the trunk of your car, drive him out to someplace far, toss him out, slit his throat and just leave his fucking ass for the buzzards " Then he turned to Nelson, "Come on, let's get him outside."

Needing no further prompting, Nelson picked up the boy and slung him roughly over his shoulder. The boy groaned painfully. With his hands and feet all tied together behind his back, being carried like that put a strain on his shoulders, but Nelson wasn't sympathetic. As he rounded the closet to exit the room, the boys head slammed against the stone wall. I winced, but Nelson just kept marching down the hall even as the boy whimpered. Gary and I followed Nelson all the way out to the front yard. Once we were near the cars, Gary got impatient. "Come on, Pouchon, open the fucking trunk."

I stepped closer to the trunk, inserted the key and popped it open. Nelson dropped the boy carelessly in and closed the lid even as he tried to scream through the gag.

"You better get going," Gary said.

I looked at him, not even trying to hide my shock. "Aren't you coming!?"

"We're coming," Gary replied, "but it's best to take two cars. Get going and we'll follow you."

Gary turned towards his car. The gate was still open. Nelson stood by to close it after us. As I got in the driver's seat, I couldn't shake the feeling that something was wrong. I put the car in gear and pulled out of our yard. It just wasn't right. In fact, it was an injustice. Not only did I have to kill the boy, but I had to drive by myself. Where was the fairness in that? As I drove along the road that led away from our secluded neighborhood, I started to get angry. That was some bullshit! Why did I have to slit the boy's throat anyway? Nelson worked for me, this was his job. The angrier I got, the harder it got to think rationally, until it became impossible. I even forgot that they were following me. Fuck them! If I had to do it then I would, but they would get a piece of my mind when I got back home. I hit the gas and sped through the narrow streets. At the corner of Delmas Road and Delmas 75 stood Quisqueya Christian School. The campus occupied a large plot of land and was surrounded by high walls. I pulled into the dark alley behind the school and turned off the engine. From inside the car, I released the trunk, then got out and went to the back of the vehicle. I lifted the boy up and tried to put him gently down on the ground, but I lost my grip and he fell face first onto the dusty ground.

"Sorry kid, I didn't mean to do that."

The boy was sobbing. His tears etched twin lines down his dirty face, but he was lying there relatively still as I considered what I was about to do. Suddenly, it occurred to me that the knife was still on the floor where we had left it. Shit! I couldn't believe we had forgotten the fucking knife! I'd have to use my Swiss army knife. That really sucked. "Okay kid, this isn't a very good night for either of us, but the sooner we get this over with, the sooner we can both get some rest."

On hearing those words, the boy struggled with all his strength. As I grabbed his head and held it tight in my left arm, I realized that this was going to be very bloody. "Look kid, it's bad enough I don't like you. But this isn't personal. Don't make it personal or it'll be much worse for you."

The kid kept struggling. Holding his head in a tight lock, I punched him several times in the side of his face, but the harder I punched him, the more he struggled. I was starting to think I should have let Nelson soften him up after all, when a pair of headlights appeared in the distance. My heart stopped. Here I was, beating a bound and gagged young boy, with the obvious intent to commit murder, the last thing I needed was a witness, but it looked like that was exactly what I had on my hands. I tried to lift the kid back into the trunk but he was struggling so much that I dropped him again.

The car sped up and was coming directly towards us. Before I could even decide what to do, it looked like the car was going to slam into us. I panicked and jumped out from behind my car. The headlights came to a screeching halt with less than ten feet to spare.

As a thick cloud of dust rolled past I heard the door open, then slam, then Gary's excited voice. "What the fuck do you think you're doing? Are you fucking crazy? You were gonna do this here, less than five miles from your fucking house?"

Nelson got out of Gary's car, approached the boy, and gave him a hard kick to the gut before picking him up and throwing him back into the trunk of the car.

Gary was furious. "Are you fucking stupid?" He looked around to make sure no one was nearby and said angrily, "Fuck this man! You want to get yourself in trouble, you go right ahead. I thought you had more fucking sense than this." Gary turned around and got back in his car. Nelson went with him and they drove off.

I stood there for a moment wondering what I should do. Realizing there was one person who could help me, I got in the car and drove to the Flamenco. I drove quickly, and even as I drove, I thought of a plan. I would take the kid out into the desert of Titanyin. It was a barren wasteland about thirty miles outside of the capital. There were several landfills out there and much that was undesirable, including unclaimed bodies from the general hospital, ended up out there. But first, I needed a gun. There was no way I would ruin my personal knife on this piece of shit in the trunk of Pop's car.

When I got to the Flamenco, all the parking spaces were free, but I parked three spaces from the entrance. I turned off the engine but I left the keys in the ignition and put the radio on full blast to mask any noise that might be coming from the trunk. The place was closed, but as I approached Max unlocked the gate and let me in. I asked him to keep an eye on my car and not let anyone near it, then I went inside.

Roland was many things. Among them, he was an ex-mercenary and a retired hit-man. But most of all, he was one of my closest friends. If anyone could get me a gun I figured it was him. But I soon learned that Roland didn't own a gun.

"Why not?" I had asked incredulously.

Roland explained that even when he did have a gun, he had to keep it completely dismantled in a locked box. That way if he ever got angry at someone, it would take him at least five minutes to find the key, unlock the box and assemble the gun. Five minutes was all he would afford anyone who pissed him off. Problem was he'd gotten so good at it that it took less than five minutes. The only solution was to get rid of the gun.

"So why do you need a gun?" he asked.

I looked around the bar to make sure there was no one within earshot. "Come with me," I told him. We walked up the stairs, out onto the street and to my car. I pointed to the trunk and said, "I have someone in there that I need to get rid of."

Roland's calm reply was as typical as his heavy French accent. "He's still alive?"

"Yep," I answered.

Roland looked at me with a raised eyebrow. "How long has he been in there?"

I looked at my watch. "Not too long, maybe twenty minutes."

"What are you gonna do with him after?" Roland asked.

"Dump him out in the desert," I replied.

Roland nodded approvingly and asked, "Have you ever killed anyone before?"

Roland's question caused me to think. "No, I've never killed before. This will be my first time."

Seeing my resolve, Roland asked, "What were you gonna use to kill him?"

I showed him my Swiss army knife, "I was gonna try with this but I don't know how. I figured it would be easier if I just shot him in the head."

Roland nodded in agreement, "Definitely. You would have to know what you are doing with that little knife, if you could do it at all." Right about then, Roland's Dominican girlfriend came out, started to dance to the Latin rhythms blaring from my car and leaned against the trunk.

"Hey get the fuck away from there!" Roland yelled. "Get your ass back inside!"

The girl went back inside, but that was when I realized I had better get the hell away from there. I thanked Roland and told him I'd think of something. He wished me luck and I drove off. I drove down Delmas Road all the way to the airport intersection. I continued past the airport to Route One, past the city limit and through the suburbs of LaPlaine. I drove until there was more and more distance between the homes, then the occasional factory appeared, then finally, open wilderness.

As I drove, I thought through what I needed to do. I'd have to use my knife after all. My knife was the biggest Swiss army knife Victorinox made, but the main blade was only four inches long. It also had a wood saw and a metal saw. I considered using the wood saw. The teeth were so aggressive that there was no doubt that it would rip through skin, flesh and tendons, but it would make a real mess and it would be painful for the boy. I wanted to get this done quickly and inflict as little pain as possible. Okay, the wood saw was Plan B. Plan A was the main blade. I had a sharpening stone, so I would make sure the blade was as sharp as possible before starting.

When I was ready, I would lay him on his stomach, get behind him, put my hand under his chin, pull his head back and slice across his throat. There was no doubt I would get blood on my hands, but I couldn't think of anything better. Hopefully, it wouldn't take more than two or three slices across the throat to get to a main blood vessel. With any luck at all, it would be over in less than a minute. Of course, there was also clean-up. I'd have to cut the shirt off the boy's body and use that to wipe my hands. If I wasn't so lucky, it would take longer and it would be even messier. In any case, it was imperative that no blood get in the car. Damn, this was getting complicated. A gun would have really made my life easier.

Once I was far out of town, I closed the windows and turned the radio off. I was listening for sounds from the trunk but I couldn't hear anything. I had driven way past the landfills and I started looking for a good place to turn off the road. I saw a small open area and pulled off into it. I turned the car around and backed carefully into the brush. The vegetation was very sparse, but one never knew what was there; the last thing I needed was a flat tire. As soon as I was sure the car was invisible from the road, I stopped.

I was about to get out when a strange feeling came over me. It wasn't a bag of garbage I was about to dispose of; it was a human being who knew beyond the shadow of a doubt that I was intent on taking his life, and he was going to fight with everything he had to stop me from doing that. He'd already been in the trunk for nearly an hour, and he might have found a way to free himself. There might even be tools in there. At the very least, there was a tire wrench. In any case, desperation would make him extremely dangerous. I stepped out of the car, then reached in and activated the trunk release. The trunk opened slowly but I couldn't hear a sound. Slowly, I circled around, careful to leave a wide space between me and the vehicle. Once I had the trunk in my line of sight, I took out my knife and opened the blade. My heart was racing. For the first time, I felt fear. After taking a deep breath, I stepped forward. I heard rustling from the trunk, but I couldn't see inside. I took one more step and in a flash, I saw the boy jump out and dash off into the wilderness. For a moment, I just stood there wondering what to do.

The image of the boy jumping out of the trunk replayed over and over in my mind. It played in slow motion until it became almost comical. The boy was like the Roadrunner escaping from the Coyote's trap. The image of the cartoon characters caused me to laugh out loud. I was laughing uncontrollably, until a sudden chill came over me. Two separate voices fought for my attention: one repeated over and over, "You would have taken the boy's life." The other just asked the question, "What always happens to the Coyote after the Roadrunner escapes?"

The voices in my head were getting louder and louder, then stopped abruptly. The sudden silence was almost supernatural: the air was still, the desert was lifeless. I listened carefully but there was nothing: no night animals; no crickets; no distant barking of stray dogs; but most importantly, no sound of running feet. The only sound I heard was the sound of my own breathing and the rapid beating of my heart.

"Oh my god! He knows he can only run so far. He thinks I'm gonna come after him. He has no idea where he is and he's desperate."

I tried to think of what I would do if I were in his place. There was no doubt: I would fight for my life; I would attack. The sudden realization the boy could come rushing at me at any moment, using anything he had as a weapon, filled me with terror. I rushed to the trunk, closed it and got into the car. Even as I was starting the engine, I had to will myself to stay calm. It wasn't until I was on the road and headed back towards town that I finally relaxed, but my nerves were frayed. I needed a drink desperately.

According to my watch, it was almost four a.m. I doubted Roland would still be at the Flamenco but it was worth a try. When I got there, Max was sleeping at his post but the lights were on. I woke up

Max and he unlocked the gate. When I got downstairs, Roland was sitting at the bar with his girlfriend. The restaurant lights were off, and the lights at the bar were set low. They were the only two in the whole place. When he saw me, Roland told his girlfriend to go upstairs. She complied immediately, but I couldn't talk to Roland yet. I went behind the bar intending to pull a Corona out of the cooler. Not finding one, I grabbed a 32-ounce Presidente. After taking a long swig, I came out from behind the bar and sat on a stool next to Roland. He could tell I needed time so he waited patiently.

When I could finally speak, I turned to Roland. "He got away man, he got away. He was in the trunk so long he found a way to untie himself. When I opened the trunk, he jumped out and ran."

Roland just shrugged his shoulders and said, "Oh well, you win some, you lose some. Don't feel bad, next time you will do better."

Unsure of what to feel or think, I just sat there frozen until the sick humor of Roland's very serious comment finally registered, and I burst out laughing. Roland laughed along with me until tears were coming out of both our eyes. Once I could speak, I put a hand on Roland's shoulder. "Hey, you think that new strip club is open?"

Roland smiled. "I'm pretty sure it is. They are the reason things were so slow for us tonight. Let's go pay them a little visit."

Roland swallowed his scotch and I took my beer with me. I finished it as we walked the block and a half to the strip club. They were still open and we drank for an hour until they closed. Roland and I walked back to the Flamenco and drank some more until about seven a.m. then I drove home.

To my surprise, the gate was open when I got home. I walked into the house and went straight to Pop's room. Gary was sitting in a chair and Pop was sitting up in bed. Both men looked as if they had seen a ghost. They were relieved to see that I was alive. Apparently, the boy had hitched a ride back into town and came back to the house. His intention was to grab some loot he had thrown over our wall and into a vacant lot the night before.

Nelson caught him and everyone assumed the kid had killed me. The boy broke down crying and swore he hadn't done anything to me, and that all he wanted was enough money for bus fare back to his hometown of Cap-Haïtien. Pop and Gary were so spooked they gave him the money. Even Nelson was so freaked out he didn't raise any objection, and they let him go.

When I heard their story, I was furious. I couldn't believe the little shit had the nerve to come back to our house after coming so close to death. The kid was obviously incorrigible and now he had been rewarded with cash! I was totally disgusted. But worse, these were the same people that left me to do all the dirty work by myself. Then when they had the kid, they not only let him go, but they paid him off! I was livid. I wanted to scream at both of them. And where the fuck was Nelson? In his room. He didn't even have the balls to face me. Fuck all of them! I stormed out of Pop's room, retired to my own and collapsed onto my bed, exhausted. It was days before I spoke to any of them.

On the night of the 11th, I went to Fritz's restaurant, Bavarian Gardens. His girlfriend Michelle, was a beautiful woman about the same size as Liz, but with Nicole's darker skin. She greeted me at the entrance of the small restaurant wearing a red, green and gold African dashiki with black accents. Her head was covered with a matching head wrap, and her jewelry consisted entirely of ebony and silver. The instant she saw me, she rushed into my arms and gave me a warm embrace. I handed her the gift I had bought for Fritz. I wasn't sure what to get so I had bought him a set of knives and hoped he would like them. Michelle led me to a table and went to get Fritz out of the kitchen.

When he came to the table, Fritz was overjoyed to see I had come. He had invited every restaurant owner on the strip, but not one of them showed up. There was a couple at another table, but the small place was basically empty. Rather than ask me what I wanted, Fritz just brought out one plate of food after another. He started with apple and potato salad, then followed up with beef stew, onion pie, sausages, sauerkraut and beef roulade. For dessert we shared a traditional German friendship cake with two candles on it, one for Fritz and one for me. The food was great and after dinner we just sat talking, joking and drinking for a few more hours.

Eventually, I got so drunk Fritz insisted on driving my car to his house and letting me crash on his couch. When I awoke the next morning, Michelle had coffee ready. Fritz was getting ready to go to the beach with Michelle and invited me to tag along, but I had to get the car back to Pop. Besides, I had a splitting headache so I went home and spent the remainder of that Sunday in bed.

There was nothing left of me. I was physically, emotionally, mentally, and spiritually drained. Incapable of any new thought, random scenes from my recent past fought to occupy the same space in my mind. Then, as I lay in bed, the ghosts of my unborn children gathered around me. A few I recognized, but the rest I didn't. I had dammed them all to eternal non-existence and at that moment, they had come to claim their father and take me away with them. I was too exhausted to struggle and besides, my place was with them. It was only fitting I be condemned to keep them company through the dull march of endless time and I was willing and ready to go until I noticed Natasha kneeling next to my bed.

She looked at me with her ever-pleading eyes and whispered that same one-word question: "Why?"

Before I could answer, the boy appeared. He knelt behind her and wrapped his arms around her naked body. As my children and I watched, he began to caress her breasts and abdomen until her head cocked back. The boy kissed her neck, tenderly at first, then with more passion. I could see beads of sweat forming on Natasha's skin as the erotic scene played out and the sounds and smells of sex filled my room. I was riveted as the two of them, oblivious to any other presence, continued on a course leading inevitably to climax. Then the boy looked at me.

I stared into his eyes, those pretty effeminate eyes, as he smiled in the most unsettling way. Suddenly, the boy's smile became a scowl and in a demonic voice he said, "Let me show you how it's done!"

He grabbed Natasha by the hair and pulled back hard. As he did, he produced a knife in his other hand and slashed across her throat. The eruption of blood covered me. It was everywhere, on my face, on my chest, it was even in my eyes and in my mouth.

I bolted upright in bed, wiping my face and spitting. Unable to see clearly, I stumbled to the door. Once I had it open, I felt my way to the bathroom and turned on the light. When I looked in the mirror I could see that my face was soaked. It wasn't blood. It was a mixture of tears, sweat and thin liquid running from my nose. I rinsed my face with cool water as I fought to catch my breath.

I went back to bed but I couldn't sleep. It was late in the night and for the first time in weeks, I wasn't under the influence of alcohol or drugs. I lay down but I was both afraid and unable to sleep. As I lay there, I sorted through the rush of thoughts. Eventually, I came to several realizations. First of all, I really had no control over my drinking. Deep down I had known it for a while but I figured I was only killing myself, so it was okay. This led me to my second realization: I had come close to killing someone, not in self-defense, but execution style, and the only reason I had almost done it was, because I had been too drunk to say no. This led me to a final realization: I needed help.

With the rising sun, I was finally able to sleep. When I awoke, it was early afternoon and I was ready to admit defeat. I was tired of the life I was living, but I didn't want to die. I picked up the phone and called Sophia, the administrative coordinator at The Agency. She had tried to tell me about a treatment center just before I went on leave, but I had told her I wasn't interested. Sophia gave me the number, but after I hung up I just stared at the phone for what seemed like an eternity. I didn't want to make the call, but I knew I had to. I thought of all the people I had hurt because of my drinking, all the lives I had affected. But it wasn't until I thought of the night in the desert that I finally picked up the phone and dialed the number.

www.ingramcontent.com/pod-product-compliance
Lightning Source LLC
LaVergne TN
LVHW011224080426
835509LV00005B/296